Censorship

Series Editor: Cara Acred

Volume 274

Independence Educational Publishers

First published by Independence Educational Publishers

The Studio, High Green

Great Shelford

Cambridge CB22 5EG

England

© Independence 2015

Photocopy licence

The material in this book is protected by copyright. However, the
purchaser is free to make multiple copies of particular articles for instructional
purposes for immediate use within the purchasing institution.
Making copies of the entire book is not permitted.

British Library Cataloguing in Publication Data

Censorship. -- (Issues ; 274)

1. Censorship.

I. Series II. Acred, Cara editor.

363.3'1-dc23

ISBN-13: 9781861687029

Printed in Great Britain

Zenith Print Group

Contents

Introduction

Censorship is Volume 274 in the **ISSUES** series. The aim of the series is to offer current, diverse information about important issues in our world, from a UK perspective.

ABOUT CENSORSHIP

You might think that censorship is a thing of the past, but you'd be wrong. Today, Twitter in Thailand, blogs in Vietnam and journalism in the Middle East are all censored. Even in the US and Europe, books, films and the Internet continue to be filtered – controlling what we see and know. However, there are instances where censorship is considered necessary, or beneficial, for example the vetting of adverts that are shown to children, or of violence on television. This book explores the many facets of censorship in today's society.

OUR SOURCES

Titles in the **ISSUES** series are designed to function as educational resource books, providing a balanced overview of a specific subject.

The information in our books is comprised of facts, articles and opinions from many different sources, including:

⇨ Newspaper reports and opinion pieces

⇨ Website factsheets

⇨ Magazine and journal articles

⇨ Statistics and surveys

⇨ Government reports

⇨ Literature from special interest groups.

A NOTE ON CRITICAL EVALUATION

Because the information reprinted here is from a number of different sources, readers should bear in mind the origin of the text and whether the source is likely to have a particular bias when presenting information (or when conducting their research). It is hoped that, as you read about the many aspects of the issues explored in this book, you will critically evaluate the information presented.

It is important that you decide whether you are being presented with facts or opinions. Does the writer give a biased or unbiased report? If an opinion is being expressed, do you agree with the writer? Is there potential bias to the 'facts' or statistics behind an article?

ASSIGNMENTS

In the back of this book, you will find a selection of assignments designed to help you engage with the articles you have been reading and to explore your own opinions. Some tasks will take longer than others and there is a mixture of design, writing and research-based activities that you can complete alone or in a group.

FURTHER RESEARCH

At the end of each article we have listed its source and a website that you can visit if you would like to conduct your own research. Please remember to critically evaluate any sources that you consult and consider whether the information you are viewing is accurate and unbiased.

Useful weblinks

www.article19.org

www.bbfc.co.uk British Board of Film Classification

www.brendanoneill.co.uk

consumers.ofcom.org.uk

www.theconversation.com

www.filmfour.co.uk

www.freedomhouse.org

www.ibtimes.com

www.indexoncensorship.org

politics.co.uk

www.rsf.org Reporters Without Borders

www.wan-ifra.org

www.yougov.co.uk.

Freedom of expression

The Universal Declaration on Human Rights (UDHR) and the International Covenant on Civil and Political Rights (ICCPR) guarantee the right to freedom of expression, both in Article 19. Freedom of expression is not only important in its own right but is also essential if other human rights are to be achieved.

For individuals

At an individual level, freedom of expression is key to the development, dignity and fulfilment of every person.

⇨ People can gain an understanding of their surroundings and the wider world by exchanging ideas and information freely with others. This makes them more able to plan their lives and to work.

⇨ People feel more secure and respected by the state if they are able to speak their minds.

For states

At a national level, freedom of expression is necessary for good government and therefore for economic and social progress.

Freedom of expression and freedom of information contribute to the quality of government in various ways:

⇨ They help ensure that competent and honest people administer the state. In a democracy, free debate about and between political parties exposes their strengths and weaknesses. This enables voters to form an opinion about who is best qualified to run the country and to vote accordingly. Media scrutiny of the Government and the Opposition helps expose corruption or other improprieties and prevents a culture of dishonesty

⇨ They promote good governance by enabling citizens to raise their concerns with the authorities. If people can speak their minds without fear, and the media are allowed to report what is being said, the Government can become aware of any concerns and address them.

⇨ They ensure that new policies and legislation are carefully considered. Through public debate, members of the public with helpful opinions on a subject can present the Government with a 'marketplace of ideas' from which to choose. Free debate about new legislation also helps ensure that the eventual law has the support of the population, making it more likely to be respected.

⇨ They promote the implementation of other human rights. They help improve government policy in all areas, including human rights. They also enable journalists and activists to highlight human rights issues and abuses and persuade the Government to take action.

For all these reasons, the international community has recognised freedom of expression and freedom of information as some of the most important human rights.

International guarantee

The right to freedom of expression is guaranteed by a number of global and regional human rights treaties, as well as under customary international law. However, this diversity of sources does not reflect a diversity of ideas about what the right means: freedom of expression is a universal right, so its meaning is largely the same in every treaty. Any differences relate mostly to how it is enforced.

The Universal Declaration of Human Rights

The Universal Declaration of Human Rights (UDHR) contains, in Article 19, the first and most widely recognised statement of the right to freedom of expression:

'Everyone has the right to freedom of opinion and expression; this right includes freedom to hold opinions without interference and to seek, receive and impart information and ideas through any media and regardless of frontiers.'

The UDHR is not a binding treaty but a recommendatory resolution adopted by the UN General Assembly. Through time and universal acceptance, however, much of the UDHR has risen to the level of customary international law, including Article 19, and is therefore binding on all states.

The International Covenant on Civil and Political Rights

The International Covenant on Civil and Political Rights (ICCPR) was meant to elaborate the UDHR and contains a more detailed but very similar statement about freedom of expression (again in Article 19):

1. Everyone shall have the right to hold opinions without interference.

2. Everyone shall have the right to freedom of expression; this right shall include freedom to seek, receive and impart information and ideas of all kinds, regardless of frontiers, either orally, in writing or in print, in the form of art, or through any other media of his choice.

3. The exercise of the rights provided for in paragraph 2 of this article carries with it special duties and

responsibilities. It may therefore be subject to certain restrictions, but these shall only be such as are provided by law and are necessary:

(a) For respect of the rights or reputations of others;

(b) For the protection of national security or of public order (ordre public), or of public health or morals.

Key aspects

As its formulation in Articles 19 of the UDHR and ICCPR shows, the right to freedom of expression is very broad in scope. It could be said to have six main aspects.

1) 'Everyone shall have the right...'

The right to freedom of expression belongs to everyone. No distinctions are permitted on the basis of someone's:

⇨ level of education

⇨ race

⇨ colour

⇨ sex

⇨ language

⇨ religion

⇨ political or other opinion

⇨ national or social origin

⇨ property

⇨ birth or any other status.

2) '...To seek, receive and impart...'

The right to impart information and ideas is the most obvious aspect of freedom of expression. It is the right to tell others what one thinks or knows in private or via the media. But freedom of expression serves a larger purpose. It enables every person to access as wide a range of information and viewpoints as possible. Known as the right to information, this includes:

⇨ reading newspapers

⇨ listening to public debates

⇨ watching the television

⇨ surfing the Internet

⇨ accessing information held by public authorities.

The right to information has emerged as a new right, distinct but inseparable from the right to freedom of expression.

3) '...Information and ideas of any kind...'

The right to freedom of expression does not just apply to information and ideas generally considered to be useful or correct. It also applies to any kind of fact or opinion that can be communicated. The UN Human Rights Committee (UNHRCm) has stressed that 'expression' is broad and not confined to political, cultural or artistic expression. It also includes controversial, false or even shocking expression. The mere fact that an idea is disliked or thought to be incorrect does not justify its censorship.

4) '...Regardless of frontiers...'

The right to freedom of expression is not limited by national boundaries. States must allow their citizens to seek, receive and impart information to and from other countries.

5) '...Through any media...'

The right to freedom of expression includes the use of any media, modern or traditional.

6) '...To respect and to ensure...'

The right to freedom of expression means that states must 'respect' free expression and not interfere with it. The right also places a positive obligation on states to actively ensure that obstacles to free expression are removed. Examples of ensuring free expression include:

⇨ ensuring that minorities can be heard

⇨ preventing the monopolisation of the media by the state or private companies.

Limitations

Most expression is completely harmless and protected under the right to freedom of expression from interference by the state.

However, 'seeking, receiving and imparting information or ideas' includes expression which few societies could tolerate, such as incitement to murder or the sale of pornography to children. As a result, freedom of expression is not absolute and can be limited when it conflicts with other rights.

International law declares freedom of expression to be the rule. Limitations are the exception, permitted only to protect:

⇨ the rights or reputations of others

⇨ national security

⇨ public order

⇨ public health

⇨ morals.

Limitation is legitimate if it falls within the very narrow conditions defined in the three-part test in Article 19(3) of the ICCPR:

1. '...Provided by law...'

The right to freedom of expression cannot be limited at the whim of a public official. They must be applying a law or regulation that is formally recognised by those entrusted with law-making.

The law or regulation must meet standards of clarity and precision so that people can foresee the consequences of their actions. Vaguely worded edicts, whose scope is unclear, will not meet this standard and are therefore not legitimate. For example, vague prohibitions on 'sowing discord in society' or 'painting a false image of the State' would fail the test.

The rationale

⇨ It is only fair that people have a reasonable opportunity to know what is prohibited, so that they can act accordingly.

⇨ A situation where officials can make rules on a whim is undemocratic. Decisions limiting human rights must be made by bodies representing the will of people.

⇨ Vague laws will be abused. They often give officials discretionary powers that leave too much room for arbitrary decision-making.

⇨ Vague laws have a 'chilling effect' and inhibit discussion on matters of public concern. They create a situation of uncertainty about what is permitted, resulting in people steering far clear of any controversial topic for fear that it may be illegal, even if it is not.

2. '...Legitimate aim...'

There must be a legitimate aim to limit the right to freedom of expression. The list of legitimate aims is not open-ended. They are provided for in Article 19(3) of the ICCPR: '...respect for the rights and reputations of others, and protection of national security, public order (ordre public), public health or morals'. They are exclusive and cannot be added to.

The rationale

⇨ Not all the motives underlying governments' decisions to limit freedom of expression are compatible with democratic government. For example, a desire to shield a government from criticism can never justify limitations on free speech.

⇨ The aim must be legitimate in purpose and effect. It is not

enough for a provision to have an incidental effect on one of the legitimate aims. If the provision was created for another reason, it will not pass this part of the test.

3. '...Necessity...'

Any limitation of the right to freedom of expression must be truly necessary. Even if a limitation is in accordance with a clear law and serves a legitimate aim, it will only pass the test if it is truly necessary for the protection of that legitimate aim. If a limitation is not needed, why impose it?

In the great majority of cases where international courts have ruled national laws to be impermissible limitations on the right to freedom of expression, it was because they were not deemed to be 'necessary'.

The rationale

⇨ A government must be acting in response to a pressing social need, not merely out of convenience. On a scale between 'useful' and 'indispensable', 'necessary' should be close to 'indispensable'.

⇨ A government should always use a less intrusive measure if it exists and would accomplish the same objective. For example, shutting down a newspaper for defamation is excessive; a retraction (or perhaps a combination of a retraction and a warning or a modest fine) would offer the victim of defamation adequate protection.

⇨ The measure must impair free expression as little as possible. It should not restrict in a broad or untargeted way, as that could interfere with legitimate expression. For example, it is too broad to ban all discussion about a country's armed forces in order to protect national security.

⇨ The impact of the measure must be proportionate and the harm that it causes to free expression must not outweigh its benefits. For example, a

limitation that provides only partial protection to someone's reputation but seriously undermines free expression is disproportionate.

⇨ A court must take into account all of the circumstances at that time before deciding to limit freedom of expression. For example, it could be legitimate to limit freedom of expression for national security reasons during a conflict but not during peacetime.

⇨ The European Convention on Human Rights (ECHR) narrows the third test by requiring limitations to be 'necessary in a democratic society'. This wording is preferable as it clarifies that the purpose of the limitation must never be to shield governments from either criticism or peaceful opposition.

What is a 'limitation' or 'restriction'?

International courts have generally judged that any action by a public body that has an actual effect on people's freedom of expression constitutes a 'restriction' or 'limitation'.

⇨ The nature of the action is irrelevant. It could be anything from a law to an internal disciplinary measure

⇨ The nature of the public body is irrelevant. It could be legislative, executive or judicial, or a publicly owned enterprise

⇨ The extent of the action's impact is irrelevant. Any discernible effect on the ability of one or more people to express themselves freely is a restriction.

The ECHR again narrows the definition of a limitation, requiring the three-part test to apply to any 'formalities, conditions, restrictions or penalties' under Article 10(2).

⇨ The above information is reprinted with kind permission from Article 19. Please visit www.article19.org for further information.

EU adopts new guidelines on freedom of expression

New guidelines were released this week by the European Union Foreign Affairs Council specifically focusing on freedom of expression online and offline.

By Alice Kirkland

A new set of guidelines laid out by the EU, and contributed to by Index on Censorship, will specifically look at freedom of expression both online and offline, and includes clauses, among others, on whistleblowers, citizens' privacy and the promotion of laws that protect freedoms of expression.

According to the Council of the European Union press statement, freedom of opinion should apply to all persons equally, regardless of who they are and where they live, affirming this freedom 'must be respected and protected equally online as well as offline'.

Significant consideration within the EU Human Rights Guidelines on Freedom of Expression Online and Offline, adopted on 12 May, is paid to whistleblowers with the council vowing to support any legislation adopted which provides protection for those who expose the misconduct of others, as well as reforming legal protections for journalists' rights to not have to disclose their sources.

Reinforcing this, the new guidelines enable the Council to help those, journalists or others, who are arrested or imprisoned for expressing their opinions both online and offline, seeking for their immediate release and observing any subsequent trials.

Member states also have an obligation to protect their citizens' right to privacy. In accordance with Article 17 of the International Covenant on Civil and Political Rights (ICCPR), the guidelines claim 'no one should be subject to arbitrary or unlawful interference with their privacy', with legal systems providing 'adequate and effective guarantees' on the right to privacy.

The guidelines will provide guidance on the prevention of violations to freedom of opinion and expression and how officials and staff should react when these violations occur. The guidelines also outline the 'strictly prescribed circumstances' that freedom of expressions may be limited; for example, operators may implement Internet restrictions (blockages, etc.) to conform with law enforcement provisions on child abuse. Laws under the new guidelines that do adequately and effectively guarantee the freedom of opinions to all, not just journalists and the media, must be properly enforced.

'Free, diverse and independent media are essential in any society to promote and protect freedom of opinion and expression and other human rights,' according to the Council press release. 'By facilitating the free flow of information and ideas on matters of general interest, and by ensuring transparency and accountability, independent media constitute one of the cornerstones of a democratic society. Without freedom of expression and freedom of the media, an informed, active and engaged citizenry is impossible.'

15 May 2014

⇨ The above information is reprinted with kind permission from Index on Censorship. Please visit www. indexoncensorship.org for further information.

Soft censorship, hard impact

A global review.

Executive summary

Soft censorship is growing alarmingly as a global phenomenon. Official 'soft censorship' (or 'indirect government censorship') describes an array of official actions intended to influence media output short of legal or extra-legal bans, direct censorship of specific content, or physical attacks on media outlets or media practitioners.

The tactics of official soft censorship are increasingly pervasive and alarmingly effective means of media manipulation and control around the world. Especially devastating in times of economic instability, governments are aware that soft censorship does not generate the international outcry evoked by killing journalists or shuttering publications. Although it is less visible, soft censorship can be equally insidious, and must be recognised for the very serious threat to media independence and press freedom it is today.

New research shows that what has long been known in Latin America as *censura sutil* or *censura indirecta* is practised in diverse forms around the world. The late Cameroonian journalist and media freedom advocate Pius Njawe observed that soft censorship is 'sophisticated repression [that] requires a sophisticated response.'

The response required to combat many elements of soft censorship is growing clearer. Synopses of incidences of soft censorship reported by human rights and press freedom groups and numerous media outlets are presented in this report. Also summarised are the findings of four recent investigations by regional experts into soft censorship in Hungary, Malaysia, Mexico, and Serbia. These reports, based on extensive research and interviews, are part of the Soft Censorship Global Review series. They were produced by the World Association of Newspapers and News Publishers (WAN-IFRA) in cooperation with the Center for International Media Assistance (CIMA), with funding of the Open Society Foundations.

A crucial first step in battling soft censorship is recognising and exposing its existence. Investigations and analyses by media, civil society groups and academics are now using corporate reports, public documents, freedom of information requests and wide-ranging interviews to reveal the extent of soft censorship in several countries. These findings are being transformed into advocacy that demands full transparency and fairness in allocation of all public funds for advertising and media support – and promotes the highest ethical professional standards for media outlets and individual media practitioners in all relations with governments at every level.

Responding to soft censorship: expose and reform

Soft censorship is used to promote positive coverage of – and to punish media outlets that criticise – officials or their actions. It is the practice of influencing news coverage of state bodies and officials and their policies and activities through allocation or withholding of state media spending (subsidies, advertising and other media contracts or assistance), or selective application of licensing, permits or regulations, to shape the broad media landscape; promote or diminish the economic viability of specific media houses or outlets; and/or reward or punish content produced by individual media workers.

These various types of soft censorship are deployed to different degrees and at different times in many countries, and are all potentially debilitating to free and independent media. Soft censorship can evoke pervasive self-censorship that restricts reporting while maintaining the appearance of media freedom.

Advertising and influence

The abusive allocation of government advertising to reward positive coverage and punish critical coverage is doubly pernicious, as taxpayer money and public wealth is used and abused to promote partisan or personal interests. The opaque and purposefully prejudiced use of official advertising subverts both media freedom and public knowledge.

Subsidies

The abusive allocation of subsidies also means that taxpayer money is used to promote partisan or private commercial interests. In numerous countries, direct subsidies distort the media landscape by propping up state media, or through biased distribution to media backing incumbent regimes.

Paid 'news'

Paid content disguised as news is a widespread form of media manipulation. Audiences are denied the honest and impartial reporting that professional journalism should supply. In many cases, arrangements formalised with media outlets institutionalise biased coverage of crucial matters.

Bribery/Payments

At the most delinquent end of the spectrum, journalists, editors and media outlets are often offered – and sometimes seek – direct payments or other compensation to shape or slant their reporting. It is a form of soft censorship often used in countries where journalists are poorly paid to favour and reward positive coverage.

Licenses, imports, audits

Several other tools and techniques are used as tools of soft censorship, although the boundaries between these and hard censorship can be indistinct or overlapping. Onerous licensing regimes are one example. Restricting access to physical means of production, such as barring import of newsprint, is another. Inspections and tax audits might be used as harassment that imposes serious costs and inconvenience on targeted media outlets or individuals, or means to shutter independent or critical voices.

Beyond the scope of the investigations detailed here are myriad forms of unofficial indirect censorship that may affect media output. These may rise from cultural, religious or other social norms and traditions, or adherence to societal narratives that influence institutional and individual reporting, and which might be promoted or imposed by a variety of non-state actors.

An early elaboration of the concept of indirect government censorship as soft censorship was offered by the Open Society Justice Initiative [OSJI – which continues to partner in these reports] in a 2005 paper that described three main forms: abuse of public funds and monopolies, abuse of regulatory and inspection powers, and extra-legal pressures. 'Indirect pressures,' the paper observed, 'combine a semblance of legality with clearly unlawful methods and goals of improperly influencing media content and other forms of political expression.'

A study of soft censorship in seven Latin American countries, *The Price of Silence: The Growing Threat of Soft Censorship in Latin America*, was issued in 2008 by the Argentine Association for Civil Rights and the OSJI. A 2009 report by the Center for International Media Assistance (CIMA) was among the first efforts to assess soft censorship as a global phenomenon.

This report builds on these and other efforts to identify and understand the bases and mechanisms of official soft censorship – and suggest means to combat it.

⇨ The above information is reprinted with kind permission from WAN-IFRA. Please visit www.wan-ifra.org for further information and full references.

Nothing should be censored – not even *Mein Kampf*

This is the text of a lecture given by Brendan O'Neil at the European Students for Liberty conference at Humboldt University in Berlin on 16 March 2014.

On 16 March, I was invited to give a lecture on the German censorship of *Mein Kampf* and the importance of freedom of speech at the European Students for Liberty conference at Humboldt University in Berlin. My speech is published below.

Many people think that freedom of speech is all about the freedom of the speaker.

They think that freedom of speech is all about the rights of the person who wants to make a speech, or publish a pamphlet, or write a book, or in some other way express his views.

And it's understandable that we think this way about freedom of speech. After all, the very name of this freedom – freedom of speech – suggests that it is wholly concerned with the right to speak, the right to say something, the right to raise your voice.

But I think the freedom to speak is only one aspect of freedom of speech. There is another aspect that tends to be overlooked.

And that is the freedom to hear – the right of everyone in society to hear or read or watch your speech and to make a moral judgement as to whether your ideas have any worth.

When we say we value freedom of speech, yes we are saying that every individual or group should be at liberty to express their views, however shocking or disturbing those views might appear. That is very important.

But we are also saying that we trust the public to be able to hear those views without going mad, without being instantly corrupted, without suffering some form of irreparable moral pollution.

We are saying that we trust ordinary people to listen to and see all kinds of ideas and imagery, and to make an independent moral decision about the value of those ideas and imagery.

Freedom of speech is only partly about your freedom to speak – it is also, just as importantly, about my right to hear you and to pass judgement on you.

And I think the main reason freedom of speech is in a bad state these days, the reason it doesn't enjoy the supreme cultural validation that it should, is because society has lost faith in that second component of freedom of speech – in the audience and its right to hear.

The corrosion of freedom of speech really speaks to a corrosion of faith in the masses, who are now looked upon, by both the left and the right, and even by many libertarians, as politically ignorant, as fickle, as easily led astray by the mass media or evil ideas, and thus they cannot be allowed to hear and see certain things.

The undermining of freedom of speech today is fuelled more by a distrust of the audience than it is by a disgust for the speaker. Without a faith in moral autonomy and political capacity, you cannot mount an effective defence of freedom of speech.

Let's consider *Mein Kampf*.

Why is this book effectively banned in Germany? It is because the German people are viewed by the authorities as intellectually untrustworthy, even as corruptible, and apparently they must be protected from this book for their own good. They must have their eyes shielded from this book in case it stirs up their inner Nazi and gives rise to another fit of far-right extremism in Germany.

The effective ban on Mein Kampf is not an attack on Hitler's rights – it is an attack on German citizens' rights, primarily their right to hear and to make independent political judgements.

The way Mein Kampf is censored is very interesting.

There isn't an actual law forbidding ownership or even sale of Mein Kampf. You can buy it in certain antique bookshops.

But it is in essence forbidden to publish a new copy of Mein Kampf and to sell this new copy in mass, mainstream bookshops.

When he died, Hitler's official place of residence was Munich. This meant that his entire state, including the copyright for Mein Kampf, passed to the government of Bavaria.

And in the 70 years since his death, the government of Bavaria, with the agreement of the federal government of Germany, has refused to grant anyone permission to publish a new version of Mein Kampf, on the basis that the book is poisonous and dangerous.

Officialdom has gone to extraordinary lengths to prevent German citizens from publishing or sharing Mein Kampf.

A few years ago, the German justice minister asked the American store Barnes & Noble to stop selling copies of the book via its website to residents of Germany.

Likewise, following an investigation by the Simon Weisenthal Center, Amazon agreed to stop distributing Mein Kampf to people with German addresses.

In 2000, the German authorities threatened legal action against the website Yahoo after it said it would auction copies of Mein Kampf and it became clear that German citizens could enter the auction.

In 2012, the British publisher Peter McGee planned to publish and distribute in Germany 100,000 copies of a pamphlet called The Unreadable Book, which would have consisted of various sections of text from Mein Kampf. But a court in Munich ruled that even publishing citations from Hitler's book violated Bavarian copyright, and so McGee backed down.

The New York Times aptly described the prevention of McGee's plans as the German authorities' 'most recent victory in a continuing battle to prevent circulation of Hitler's seminal work'.

This is blatant censorship.

When German citizens are blocked from ordering books online, when publishers are prevented from quoting Hitler in pamphlets, there is clearly something deeply political and censorious at work. The German authorities are attempting to deprive their citizens of access to a particular literary work. That is censorship.

The justification offered for this censorship, even though it's never called that, is that if Mein Kampf were freely available It would offend those who suffered under the Nazi regime and more importantly it might stoke and inflame neo-Nazi and far-right sentiment.

From this perspective, the restrictions on Mein Kampf should be seen as an assault on the autonomy of currently alive German citizens rather than on the freedom of the long-dead Hitler.

For the ban on Mein Kampf is justified on the basis that its content might generate instability by warping and twisting German people's minds, reigniting the racist outlook. In short, German people cannot be trusted to have free access to this book. Their minds are so malleable, and their souls so corruptible, that they apparently require the authorities to protect them from an old mad, ranting text.

How patronising. How insulting. In keeping with all modern-day acts of censorship, the real target of the restrictions on Mein Kampf isn't

the author himself; it's the public, who have been judged too morally immature to be able to cope with seeing this book.

Their right to read, to think, to argue, to make an independent judgment call as to whether this book has any moral worth, has been denied.

There is a terrible irony to Germany's censorship of Mein Kampf – it is presented as an anti-Hitler measure, but it actually rehabilitates one of Hitler's most foul ideas: namely that some books are so morally and politically corrupting that they must be banned/burned.

Censorship is always, at root, an attack on the public.

This was recognised by the great 18th-century radical Thomas Paine, who said censorship of published material is more of a 'sentence on the public [than] the author', because it effectively tells the public 'they shall not think, they shall not read'.

That sentencing of the public, that assault on the public's rights, has come to the fore even more starkly in cases of censorship in recent years.

Today, censorship is primarily justified on the basis that the public is fragile or stupid and therefore it cannot be trusted with certain printed or broadcast material.

Today, the question of 'who' might have access to the published material under consideration, the question of the audience's presumed levels of intelligence, is always at the forefront in attempts to impose censorship and in successful impositions of censorship.

Consider the current feminist campaign in Britain to rid The Sun of Page 3 – that famous page in Britain's best-known tabloid which every day features a half-naked lady.

It isn't nakedness per se, or women's breasts, that these feminist censors want banned. They accept the exposure of breasts in movies, and some of them are the very same people who campaigned for the right of women to publish photos of themselves breastfeeding on Facebook. No, it's the 'audience' for Page 3 that makes them uncomfortable and censorious – an audience that is largely working class, male, blue collar.

When anti-Page 3 campaigners say Page 3 increases misogyny, and even leads to violence and rape, what they are really saying is that the audience for this imagery is animalistic; this audience is like attack dogs who hear a word or see an image and thoughtlessly respond to it.

It's not the content that offends these censorious campaigners; they accept the right of people to expose and depict breasts; it's the audience that offends them.

Or consider, on the other side of the political spectrum, those European right-wingers, including some people who hilariously describe themselves as libertarians, who suggest we should ban the Koran

on the basis that it's a corrupting, immoral book.

Again, it isn't the content that offends them. After all, the Christian Bible also contains its fair share of strange claims and ideas that are ill-suited to the 21st century. No, it's the audience for the Koran that drives these right-wingers to embrace arguments for censorship. Muslim immigrants with apparently febrile, shaky minds, easily led into violence – it is fear of these people rather than fear of the Koran per se that motors the desire for anti-Koranic censorship.

Censorship is demanded not because the content is uniquely terrible, but because the audience for it is presumed to be a lower form of intellectual life than us, than the educated, the erudite, the right-thinking,

All the main forms of censorship today are informed by a view of the public as dumb and dangerous.

So campaigners calling for the outlawing of hate speech that offends

women or minorities do so on the basis that it can create a climate of poisonous hatred, even violence, and can cause real world violence and mayhem. That is, the public will hear these words and be corrupted by them, made automatically violent.

Or consider the expansion of the definition of incitement. Once, the word 'incitement' was used to refer specifically to one person directly inciting another to commit a criminal act, usually an imminent criminal act.

Now, even criticism of Islam can be referred to as 'incitement to hatred'. The offensive chanting of football fans is talked about as 'incitement to violence'.

The broadening of the definition of incitement, and the corresponding clampdown on allegedly inciting speech, sums up the key problem with censorship today: it is driven by a view of an instant, will-free relationship between words and actions; between what is written and how people behave. It calls into question people's ability to think, exercise free will, and determine whether and how to respond to particular ideas. The claim that words incite is as much a demonisation of the public and its mental capacities as it is a criminalisation of certain words and ideas.

Your position on freedom of speech and whether it is a good thing really reveals a lot about how you view humanity and whether you think humanity is a good thing. This has always been the case.

So it is not a coincidence that the true demand for freedom of speech emerged as the modern democratic sensibility took shape, in the 17th, 18th and 19th centuries.

A growing trust in man's ability to run his own life, select his own leaders and determine his nation's fate naturally went hand in hand with a growing trust in man's ability to discuss, debate, to hear all sorts of good, bad, weird and outrageous things and to 'decide' if they are right or wrong.

So John Milton, in the 17th century, said we should let truth and falsehood grapple in the public arena, and truth, he said, will win out. In short, the public sphere is more than capable

of working out right from wrong, good from bad.

Thomas Paine, in the 18th century, said the following: 'When opinions are free, in either matters of religion or politics, truth will finally and powerfully prevail.' That is, the freer discussion is, the more the public has access to claims and ideas, the more likely enlightenment becomes.

In the 19th century, the great liberal John Stuart Mill said 'complete liberty of contradicting and disproving our opinion is the very condition which justifies us in assuming its truth…'. That is, it is only by submitting your ideas or beliefs to the rigours of public discussion and public ridicule that you can be sure they are correct, true, right. Public deliberation – that is, the public – will decide if you are right.

Past liberals and democrats had such faith in humankind that, unlike the rulers who came before them, and the ones who dominate today, they were willing to let it be the referee of the great battles of meaning and ideology.

Today, the opposite is the case. Today, it is the collapse of trust in mankind that leads to the undermining of free speech, which leads to demands for the audience to be protected from foul words and destabilising ideas.

Misanthropy, not politics, is the key driver of censorship in the 21st century,

On both the left and the right, thinkers and campaigners now doubt the capacities of the public. Some on the left campaign to ban hate speech, far-right propaganda, sexist language, and so on, because they believe such things might warp us. And some on the right want to clamp down on Islamist preachers, 'sympathy for terrorism', and other ideas and arguments that they think will warp fragile sections of society.

Even among libertarians, an outward defence of freedom of speech constantly rubs up against an inward disdain for the moral autonomy and mental capacities of the public.

At this very conference, I have attended sessions and heard discussions on the problem of public ignorance, on wether we need expert cliques to run aspects of public life that the public doesn't understand, about the problem of the mass media and its harmful impact on people's minds and belief systems.

So even libertarians who challenge censorship also help to fuel the *logic* of modern censorship – which is that the public is ill-equipped for full and frank free debate.

They claim to be libertarian in one breath, but in the next they implicitly call into question the very foundation of liberty – namely the conviction that human beings are capable of autonomy, of thought, of moral consideration and action, and they do not require experts or priests to tell them what is right and what is wrong.

To defend freedom of speech today, we must, of course, stand up for every individual or group facing censorship. But we must go further than that – we must also recover and resuscitate faith in mankind's moral capacities. We must challenge misanthropy, because freedom of speech is impossible in a society that fears humanity itself.

So yes, let us unban Mein Kampf, not because we like Hitler or his ideas, but because we trust that people can think for themselves and are capable of knowing and understanding what is good and what is wicked.

16 March 2014

⇨ The above information is reprinted with kind permission from Brendan O'Neil. Please visit www.brendanoneil.co.uk for further information.

Books that have been banned:

Lady Chatterly's Lover, by D H Lawrence.
Banned from 1928 to 1960.

All Quiet on the Western Front, by Erich Maria Remarque.
Banned by the Nazi government in 1933.

Doctor Zhivago, by Boris Pasternak.
Banned in the former Soviet Union until 1988.

The Wonderful Wizard of Oz, by L Frank Baum.
Banned in numerous US libraries and schools in the 1930s and 1950s.

1984, by George Orwell.
Banned by the American Libraries Association and in the USSR.

The Diary of Anne Frank, by Anne Frank.
Banned in Lebanon and the subject of censorship debate in Michigan, US, in 2013.

The DaVinci Code, by Dan Brown.
Banned in Lebanon in 2004.

Rowan Atkinson: we must be allowed to insult each other

Rowan Atkinson has launched a campaign for a change in the law that bans 'insulting words and behaviour'.

The *Blackadder* and *Mr Bean* star attacked the 'creeping culture of censoriousness' which has resulted in the arrest of a Christian preacher, a critic of Scientology and even a student making a joke, it was reported.

He criticised the 'new intolerance' as he called for part of it the Public Order Act to be repealed, saying it was having a 'chilling effect on free expression and free protest'.

Mr Atkinson said: 'The clear problem of the outlawing of insult is that too many things can be interpreted as such. Criticism, ridicule, sarcasm, merely stating an alternative point of view to the orthodoxy, can be interpreted as insult.'

Police and prosecutors are accused of being over-zealous in their interpretation of Section 5 of the Act, which outlaws threatening, abusive and insulting words or behaviour, the *Daily Mail* reported.

What constitutes 'insulting' is not clear. It has resulted in a string of controversial arrests.

They include a 16-year-old boy being held for peacefully holding a placard reading 'Scientology is a dangerous cult', and gay rights campaigners from the group Outrage! detained when they protested against Islamic fundamentalist group Hizb ut-Tahrir over its stance on gays, Jews and women.

Mr Atkinson said he hoped the repeal of Section 5 would pave the way for a move to 'rewind the culture of censoriousness' and take on the 'outrage industry – self-appointed arbiters of the public good encouraging outrage to which the police feel under terrible pressure to react'.

Speaking at the Westminster launch of the campaign, he added: 'The law should not be aiding and abetting the new intolerance.'

He was joined by Lord Dear, former Chief Constable of West Midlands Police, and former Shadow Home Secretary David Davis.

Mr Davis said: 'The simple truth is that in a free society, there is no right not to be offended. For centuries, freedom of speech has been a vital part of British life, and repealing this law will reinstate that right.'

The campaign has united an unlikely coalition of support including The Christian Institute and The National Secular Society as well as Big Brother Watch, The Freedom Association and The Peter Tatchell Foundation.

18 October 2012

⇨ The above information is reprinted with kind permission from *The Telegraph*. Please visit www.telegraph.co.uk for further information.

Children of the Internet: free speech in the digital age

By Nishith Hedge

Unlike any previous time in the history of the world, there is a generation growing up today with unprecedented knowledge and power at their immediate and constant disposal. Their voices cannot be silenced, they can communicate with each other instantaneously from anywhere in the world. They are children of the Internet, and they are politically and socially empowered in ways that are not yet clearly understood. Increasingly defining their identities online as much as offline, net-powered Millenials are collectively reshaping social norms – defining the legacy their generation will leave society. The Internet is a product of, and a critical factor in, this legacy.

For example, the Internet is a key medium for personal expression. Deliberately open-access and open-source architectures that transcend national boundaries means that the online world is a place where its users become increasingly accustomed to possessing both a platform and a voice regardless of their status in society. Even where it is dangerous to criticise politicians, or to practise a faith, or to be homosexual, the Internet provides shelter in anonymity and the chance to meet like-minded people. In this way, the children of the Internet have access to support, advice and assistance, but also to allies. Even the most isolated human can now take action with the power of a collaborative collective rather than as a lone individual, and they do so with an attitude that has become acclimatised to unfettered freedom of speech.

For the Internet generation, this translates to their political actions online and often erupts into their offline behaviour, too. Online petitions gain infinitely more traction than their pen-and-paper twins, and the more anarchic side of the Internet takes no prisoners in parodying public figures, as evinced recently with the numerous revisions of the recent 'beer and bingo' tax cut advertisements produced by the ruling coalition. More controversially, Wikileaks infamously released hundreds of thousands of classified government communiqués, and 'hacktivist' groups such as Anonymous make their presence felt with powerful retaliations against firms and governments that they perceive to have suppressed Internet freedom. Even high-security sites such as the US Copyright Office and Paypal have been targeted – civil disobedience that is symptomatic of the new, sharing Internet generation that is paradoxically mindful of personal privacy and disparaging of public opacity.

For the strongest demonstration of the way this attitude and power translates, look no further than the violent reaction of a primarily young body of protesters during the Arab Spring and in Ukraine. The Internet was the conduit through which popular campaigns against ruling regimes transformed into widespread civil disobedience and a full-blown political movement. Empowered with access to forms of political commentary comparatively free of governmental intervention and the ability of every protester to act as a professional journalist by virtue of a camera phone and a Twitter account, the children of the Internet communicated, mobilised and acted to cast away governments from Tunisia to Yemen; Egypt twice over. They made their voices heard: not at the ballot box as previous generations might have, but in the streets of Cairo and Sana'a and the virtual spaces of Facebook and Blackberry Messenger. Small wonder then, that governments targeted and blocked social networking sites to quell dissent. In many countries the Internet was shut down altogether.

Yet, the Internet persevered – as John Gilmore, co-founder of the Electronic Frontier Foundation noted: 'The Internet treats censorship as a malfunction and routes around it.' Despite the long running tussle between the users of the Internet and governments who seek to regulate it, it remains untameable. In each instance, almost immediately after Internet usage has been restricted, information has circulated about circumventing government regulations – even total shutdowns have been dodged through external satellite connections.

Powered overwhelmingly by the young, the Internet is changing the way our societies are structured. Its effects upon our civilisation are poorly understood, particularly among young people who have never known a world without the Internet. Ultimately, however, it has done more for individual freedom than any other development in the last half-century. It grants any person a voice with mere access to a keyboard and a broadband connection. It holds governments to account in new and innovative ways, and most crucially, it is an irreversible development. An entire generation defines itself, subconsciously, through the Internet; previous such advancements came only through the invention of the printing press, radio and television. One thing is for certain – as broadband usage approaches saturation in many developed countries, we are all children of the Internet now.

2 June 2014

⇨ The above information is reprinted with kind permission from Index on Censorship. Please visit www.indexoncensorship.org for further information.

Digital age ratings

How can I choose appropriate films and TV for my family to watch online on their computers, tablets, games console and smartphones?

The BBFC works with a number of on demand services to provide trusted age ratings for video content available for download and streaming online. Age ratings for online content are not required by law, but are used voluntarily through a service launched by the BBFC in collaboration with the home entertainment industry in 2008. Some platforms also provide parental controls allowing parents to make available to their children films with an appropriate age rating for them. The BBFC and home entertainment industry recognise that this is helpful to parents when both they and their children are selecting film or TV content to stream or download.

Why are digital age ratings useful?

Providing BBFC age ratings for online content allows viewers to make the same informed viewing and purchasing choices for themselves and their families when using Digital Video Services, as they do when visiting the cinema or renting or buying DVDs and Blu-ray.

In 2011 the BBFC commissioned some research which showed a public demand for the same BBFC ratings to be available for online content as for DVDs and Blu-rays in shops and for films at the cinema. The research found that 82% of parents prefer to download films that are classified with the trusted BBFC age ratings, symbols and BBFCinsight information. This research is available on the BBFC research page www.bbfc.co.uk/what-classification/research.

Online services and other places using BBFC age ratings

The BBFC age ratings can be found on a number of Video-on-Demand platforms, content producers, film studios and airlines. These include:

Services

Barnes & Noble – Nook

BFI Player

Blinkbox

Blackberry

BT Vision

Curzon Home Cinema

Find Any Film

Hopster

iTunes

Kaleidescape

Knowhow Movies

Microsoft – Xbox Video, Windows Phone, Windows 8

Netflix

Picturebox

Sainsbury's Entertainment

Sony Entertainment Network

TalkTalk

Tesco Clubcard TV

The Horror Show

UltraViolet

Wuaki.tv

Airlines

British Airways

Monarch

Thomson

Virgin Atlantic

Mobile content

The Mobile Broadband Group has appointed the BBFC to take over from the Independent Mobile Classification Board (IMCB) in providing the independent framework that underpins the Mobile Operators' code of practice, established in 2004, for the self-regulation of content on mobile.

The Classification Framework defines content that is unsuitable for customers under the age of 18 and is based on the BBFC's Classification Guidelines for film and video.

The self-regulatory partnership between the mobile operators and the BBFC bring trusted, transparent and consistent BBFC standards to bear on content accessed via mobile networks. It protects children by restricting adult content to adults only. The Classification Framework is a living document which is updated regularly to reflect evolving public attitudes and societal concerns.

The Classification Framework has been developed using the BBFC's Classification Guidelines. The Guidelines are based on large scale public consultations involving around 10,000 people, and are revised every four to five years.

The Classification Framework enables commercial content providers to self-classify their mobile commercial content as either suitable or unsuitable for users under 18. The Classification Framework will also be used to calibrate the filters used by the Operators to restrict access to Internet content via mobile networks by those under 18 to the extent technically possible.

2014

⇨ The above information is reprinted with kind permission from BBFC. Please visit www.bbfc.co.uk for further information.

Case study

Website

britainfirst.org

Issue

The mobile network operators contacted the BBFC for advice following a complaint they had received from the website owner that the site was placed behind the network operators' adult filters despite containing no content which, in the opinion of the complainant, would require it to be restricted to adults only.

Adjudication

The BBFC viewed the content of the website on 29 and 30 April 2014.

We concluded that the website falls within scope of the Classification Framework.

We noted that the website contained views which could be regarded as racist.

Material on the website espouses taking the law into Britain First's own hands, plainly stating that the police are not doing a good job dealing with what the group judges to be a Muslim threat to the British way of life. Among the publications on the site, there are references to the 'Islamic invader' and a 'horrendous epidemic of sexual abuse ... ruining countless children's lives' perpetrated by 'the Muslim paedophile'. While some of this content is based on recent criminal cases, the publications suggest that such behaviour is endemic in the Muslim community.

Having looked at the website we concluded that it would confound public expectations and be unacceptable to broad public opinion if we were to classify the site lower than 18. We would therefore classify the site at 18.

Anonymity will be the next victim of Internet censorship

An article from The Conversation.

By Erke Boiten, Senior Lecturer, School of Computing and Director of Interdisciplinary Cyber Security at University of Kent

THE CONVERSATION

The worrying developments in UK Internet freedom over the last year make predictions for 2014 gloomy to say the least. Censorship now affects us all, so we should be thinking about it. And it's not politically driven censorship we should be most afraid of.

This year has been characterised by tension between the UK Government's use of terrorism laws and free speech and, more recently, by concern over the unavoidable over-blocking of content in the name of protection. Yet there are greater threats to our Internet freedom than the heavy hand of the Government.

Oversight versus interference

Both the Government and Internet service providers have abdicated responsibility for the quality control of the security filters being put in place in a bid to prevent children from accessing pornographic content at home.

ISPs such as BT and Sky have delegated the task of deciding what to block to third-party companies. For accountability and oversight that is bad news but in terms of possible political interference it is actually good.

Why censorship?

There have been three main drivers for Internet censorship. One is child abuse imagery, the banning of which is in line with the general population's views. Websites containing child porn can be taken down, for example through the Internet Watch Foundation, and, since November, search engines have returned warnings and reduced results when certain terms have been searched for. Although porn in general is not illegal, the ISPs' filters will have an impact on the blocking of child abuse by negatively affecting the distribution of borderline illegal material.

The second driver is combating extremism. It is still unclear how censorship will be applied here, but classification is highly problematic. No clear public mandate exists for this censorship, nor are links with legislation on issues such as hate speech or proscription of organisations, made explicit. In its filters, BT does not have an 'extremism' category, although some content may fall within its 'weapons and violence' or 'hate' labels.

The final category is media organisations aiming to protect their copyright. The 2010 Digital Economy Act allows for ISPs to apply sanctions (such as bandwidth restriction and disconnection) to users who have downloaded copyrighted material. ISPs have also been forced to block file-sharing websites, such as The Pirate Bay and BT includes the practice in its filtering. But file sharing isn't always illegal and even when it is, public opinion is divided about whether or not it is acceptable. The heavy-handed measures that can be taken show the impact of the commercial interests in this domain.

Mission creep

It's important to note that BT is filtering in 14 categories, even though David Cameron promised nothing broader than 'porn' filters. The generous explanation for this is that the third-party providers being used by ISPs already had a range of filtering options in place for parental controls or use in schools, for example filtering against high bandwidth activities like file sharing and media streaming.

More worryingly though, it has been reported that the BT filters also restrict access to sites promoting the use of proxies. This is where the next battle over Internet censorship will be fought. Restricting the technological means through which Internet users can obscure their IP addresses, obtain some anonymity, and hide the content they are accessing from others is the next big target.

Again, the excuse may be that the third party providers already have this built into their products for good reasons. In the context of school web filters, for example, circumvention of filters needs to be prevented.

But it looks like these measures could well be broadened. The IWF and the Child Exploitation and Online Protection Centre have been asked to investigate child abuse imagery in the 'Dark Web'. The only predictable, and sensible, recommendation for reducing child porn to come out of this will be to restrict access to the Dark Web. And that has to be done by restricting a user's ability to disguise their activities.

Media companies and the TTIP

This by itself will not cause the UK Government to restrict access to Tor, VPNs, or proxies in general. However, the media copyright lobby will want to make this happen because peer-to-peer networks, content indexed through torrent sites, possibly using some form of anonymous routing along the way, carry the majority of the 'illegal' file-sharing load.

Media companies stand to gain significant powers, possibly trumping national legislation, through trade agreements such as TTIP. Using these, they will want to close off all avenues of illegal file sharing, and they are unlikely to care about collateral damage to Internet privacy. Thus, we have to worry about restrictions on the use of Tor anonymous routing, VPNs, proxies, and any other ways that allow us to be more anonymous and protected on the Internet.

This prediction then brings together the two big Internet freedom storylines of the last six months. The Government's desire for quick Internet censorship solutions will end up impeding our capacity to defend ourselves against overzealous surveillance from intelligence services and tech companies.

The Tor fightback

The good news is that Tor traffic has proved hard to detect and shut down. Many countries have tried and failed. Security companies claiming to have the required technology typically are only able to block older versions.

These days, Tor connections look like normal secure web traffic. Currently only China systematically and openly blocks Tor (with its Great Firewall) for long periods of time. They do this by blocking the eight 'directory authorities' that form the entry point to Tor, in combination with Deep Packet Inspection. In response, the Tor project continually develops new camouflage methods, and also very promising tools for detecting Internet censorship. It is very sad that we may be using this tool sometime soon in the UK, and that Russia and Japan have been reported to be considering blocking Tor. All is not lost, but we should be on our guard.

20 December 2013

⇨ The above information is reprinted with kind permission from The Conversation. Please visit www.theconversation.com for further information.

Pianist Dejan Lazic demands bad review be removed from Google under EU 'right to be forgotten' ruling

The Washington Post *were not impressed by the classical musician's request – so they published a counter-article containing his emails.*

By Jenn Selby

Disgruntled classical pianist Dejan Lazic probably wasn't expecting an entire article in response to his request for a 2010 review on his performance to be removed under the European Union 'right to be forgotten' ruling.

But then, *The Washington Post* weren't expecting such an ask from the Croatian-born maestro either – the first of its kind the publication has ever received.

The original review was written by critic Anne Midgette. The *Post* described her words on Lazic as 'tepid' and 'peppered' with citations on his achievements.

'Not eviscerating,' they write. 'Not a "slam" But a criticism, sure.'

Unfortunately for Lazic, it appears top of the first page of his Google results. So he used the EU ruling in order to demand that it be permanently deleted from the Internet.

'To wish for such an article to be removed from the Internet has absolutely nothing to do with censorship or with closing down our access to information,' the *Post* quotes his email to them as reading.

Instead, Lazic argued, he should have the right to control 'the truth' of his own public image.

'It's a question that goes far beyond law or ethics, frankly – it's also baldly metaphysical, a struggle with the very concept of reality and its determinants,' the *Post* writes in response to the request.

'Lazic (and to some extent, the European court) seem to believe that the individual has the power to determine what is true about himself, as mediated by the search engines that process his complaints.'

The piece goes on to suggest that Lazic's ask demonstrates how the ruling might be misinterpreted and potentially misused in the future.

Under the current ruling, removed articles can be deleted from the European search engine, but cannot be got rid of from the worldwide web entirely.

'We ought to live in a world, Lazic argues, where everyone – not only artists and performers but also politicians and public officials – should be able to edit the record according to their personal opinions and tastes,' the *Post* concludes.

'This is all in pursuit of some higher, objective truth.'

2 November 2014

⇨ The above information is reprinted with kind permission from The Independent. Please visit www.independent.co.uk for further information.

Forget the right to be forgotten, other means exist

An article from The Conversation.

By David Haynes, Visiting Lecturer at City University London

THE CONVERSATION

The May 2014 ruling by the European Court of Justice, dubbed the right to be forgotten, is seen as a precedent for all Internet searches in all European Union member states. But the issues this ruling tries to address could be better dealt with using practices that exist.

The implications of the ruling are that publishers do not have to redact history by removing personally embarrassing or inconvenient reports from their web pages or online archives. Instead, search results to those pages will be removed.

Google has responded by putting a general disclaimer at the bottom of results pages for such searches: 'Some results may have been removed under data protection law in Europe'. This implies that links have been deleted from a personal name search, even when this is not the case. It also implies that other searches are not modified in some way. But neither of two implications are quite true.

Eli Pariser in his book *The Filter Bubble: What the Internet is Hiding From You* talks about instances where two individuals with a similar demographic do an identical search and get very different results. This 'filtering' of results is a normal part of the profiling of individual searchers and tailoring of results to accord with their preferences or worldview.

Google tries to arbitrate on each request under the 'right to be forgotten' rather than referring the matter to the data protection regulators in EU member states. Individuals can complete a form on the Google website where they can identify themselves, identify the web pages that are problematical, and give reasons for requesting removal of the links. This has opened the floodgates and in the first five weeks Google has had 250,000 requests from 70,000 people to remove links.

The right to be forgotten also raises questions about freedom of information, privacy and rehabilitation of offenders. Taken together they show that such a law is ineffective when other means to deal with libel or privacy issues exist.

For instance, few would deny that it is in the public interest to maintain links between the name of a public individual such as a politician or senior official and factual news reports in the press. Inconvenient past statements and behaviour should be a matter of public record and officials and politicians should be accountable, even if their attitudes have since changed.

But public figures are also people. And people have human rights including the 'right to a private and family life'. Trying to maintain privacy raises practical difficulties in taking down material that is no longer relevant or up to date.

Once something has been published there is an absurdity in trying to 'unpublish' it, especially when there are alternative legal remedies to deal with breaches of trust or libel. In the Max Mosley case damages of £60,000 were awarded against the *News of the World* in 2008 for breach of privacy following publication of a story based on a secret video of sexual nature. It demonstrated that libel laws and press regulation can be used to address privacy concerns and that additional privacy legislation is probably not necessary.

Finally, there is a powerful principle of reintegrating offenders into the community. This requires some kind of forgiveness by society once a sentence has been served. For instance, if an ex-offender is applying for a job, in the UK they do not have to declare spent convictions. The law does not allow employers to discriminate against them, if for instance they discover details of a spent conviction from an Internet search about the candidate.

The other side of the argument is that perhaps the employer has the right to know the history of an employee. Employers should be able to form their own view on the suitability of a candidate in light of all relevant information, rather than having their access to information restricted.

It is not possible to rewrite history. Once something has been said, it cannot be 'unsaid'. This is particularly true in the digital world, where there is effectively no control over the distribution or storage of information that has appeared on the Internet. While respecting individual rights, we must balance this against public accountability and use existing remedies for dealing with inaccuracies, breaches of confidentiality, and discrimination. Perhaps the right to be forgotten should really have been forgotten in the interests of a more practical, just and workable data protection regime in Europe.

14 July 2014

⇨ The above information is reprinted with kind permission from The Conversation. Please visit www.theconversation.com for further information.

The Internet censorship programme you're not allowed to know about

By Jane Fae

If you thought filtering of terror-related sites was no more than an unfulfilled gleam in the eyes of the Home Office, think again. They've been doing it for the best part of five years.

The announcement last autumn about how home Internet access might soon be subject to such filtering is not some new initiative, but an extension of one with a significant track record.

Over the past few months, the focus has been on controls being applied to domestic Internet. These are, at present, two-fold. There is the Cleanfeed, which serves to block access to a list of child abuse sites maintained by the Internet Watch Foundation (IWF), as well as, controversially, a lengthening list of sites which are alleged to encourage digital piracy. And there are the various filtering options that domestic Internet service providers (ISPs) have opted for in response to government demands that they save us all from a deluge of online smut.

The set-up with regards to mobile phone filtering and public Wi-Fi is not dissimilar: local UK-based service providers backed by mostly non-UK filters.

There is, however, a fourth channel of access to the Internet – and it is here that police and the Home Office have been intervening to prevent the public from accessing material they believe to be terror-related. This is public estate Internet: in schools and universities, hospitals and government buildings. And unlike other Internet channels, it's filtered by a mix of companies, including many that are UK-based.

To piece the story together, you need to put together various freedom of information requests and parliamentary responses. This is what you get at the end of it:

⇨ Between November 2008 and February 2011, the Labour Government ran a pilot project where sites identified as hosting material in contravention of existing terror laws would be blocked to 'public estate' access.

⇨ Sites were flagged up by the police initially and, since 2010, by the Counter Terror Internet Referrals Unit (CTIRU), passed to the Crown Prosecution Service (CPS) for evaluation, and then fed to filtering software companies.

⇨ Following a pause for evaluation between February 2011 and June 2011, the project re-commenced in July 2011.

⇨ According to official government statements, since 2010 some 5,700 UK-based sites have been taken down, while some 1,000 overseas sites have been filtered.

The Home Office said: 'The focus has been on voluntary end-user filtering. Unlike blocking, which occurs at the network level and over which users have no choice, filtering software allows end users to choose to apply filtering at the desktop level.

'The filtering list is provided to companies who supply filtering products across the public estate, including schools and libraries... There is no formal appeal process but if there is concern regarding the filtering of a specific URL containing illegal material, contact should be made with Home Office'.

So much the Home Office are happy to confirm. However, in respect of what sites are on the list and which companies are doing the filtering, it is rather more reticent.

Over the past three years, TJ McIntyre, a lecturer in law at University College Dublin has doggedly sought answers to a number of questions using freedom of information legislation.

His pursuit boils down to three questions: which sites are being filtered, which companies are doing the filtering and what liabilities would these companies incur if they filtered a site in error?

To date, he has had little success. To most of his questions, the Home Office initially cited exemptions on grounds of law enforcement and national security. When McIntyre challenged this refusal, an official review agreed that the rejection had been over-hasty and that the Home Office had erred. Not, that is, by failing to answer his question: but by citing the wrong reason for doing so.

We do know the name of one UK company that was involved in filtering alleged terror sites. In a parliamentary answer given back in April 2009, Vernon Coaker, then a minister at the Home Office, revealed that one of the companies carrying out such filtering was Smoothwall. However, he declined to provide a fuller list. The Home Office has since cited fears that UK companies might be subject to DOS (denial of service) and other attacks if their participation in this scheme were revealed.

It is unlikely that we will learn, any time soon, who is taking part in this 'voluntary' scheme – or what they are blocking – although this is not an issue because, again according to the Home Office: 'All material filtered from the public estate is... considered to be illegal under the Terrorism Act 2006, as assessed by the Crown Prosecution Service (CPS)'.

That assertion is questionable – on a couple of counts. In July 2013 – just a few days after the

CTIRU owned up to having filtered 1,000 sites, the CPS claimed: 'The scheme has so far seen the review by specialist prosecutors in CTD [counter-terrorism division] of more than 50 submissions from CTIRU'.

This suggests that perhaps not all sites added to the filtering list are reviewed by the CPS.

It also raises further questions over the censorship involved. When it comes to obscenity, the UK already operates a system of prior restraint through the back door: films are routinely censored, by the British Board of Film Classification, on the basis of how the CPS interpret the Obscene Publications Act. Such assertions have rarely been tested in court and, when they are, the CPS does not always win. It is therefore equally possible that the CPS' evaluation of whether a site would breach the Terror Act 2006 is also open to challenge.

There is also the matter of jurisdiction. Back when the Government was arguing the need for a new law on possession of extreme porn, the Home Office was arguing very clearly that the obscene publications law was inadequate because it could not be used to block websites hosted abroad. New legislation was therefore needed and duly passed.

So despite re-assurances from Home Office and CPS, it is not unthinkable that they could make mistakes. This is precisely what happened in 2008, when two academics – Rizwaan Sabir and Hicham Yezza – were arrested and held for six days for possession of a 'terror training manual', which was widely available as an academic study tool.

If the owner of a website ever did find out they had been blocked, who is liable – and to what extent?

This question is important, given the announcement last autumn by then-crime and security minister James Brokenshire that government is preparing to require broadband companies to block extremist websites. That announcement also talked of empowering 'a specialist unit' – possibly the CTIRU – to identify and report content that fell within this category.

That is problematic on several grounds. As already highlighted, the main broadband companies use filter providers that are not UK-based: the tangle of a UK police unit providing a list to overseas companies which is then fed back to UK ISPs is a liability nightmare.

The alternative and somewhat neater option is to feed such websites back through Cleanfeed. The danger of such an approach, however, is that the Cleanfeed system has been defended against its staunchest critics on the grounds it is only ever intended to be used in respect of blocking child abuse material. A number of child protection experts have expressed fears that using Cleanfeed in this way could seriously damage child protection in the UK.

It is against this background, therefore, that we now await the result of a first tier tribunal appeal by TJ McIntyre which took place last week. This appeal is against the Home Office decision not to allow him to view Home Office material on the possible liability they and/or filtering companies would face for wrongful blocking.

So far, the Home Office have claimed that the only relevant material is contained in the licence agreement with those companies. According to McIntyre: 'That makes me think that there is some form of indemnity in place whereby the Home Office promises to pay any damages that might be incurred by the companies if the Home Office wrongfully designates a site to be

blocked. But of course we don't know that for sure.'

The result of that appeal is expected shortly. Depending on the outcome, we might soon be finding out a lot more about the shape of Internet filtering to come – and whether the Home Office is secretly indemnifying UK companies against the costs of acting unlawfully.

Jane Fae is a feminist and campaigner on issues of political and sexual freedom. You can follow her on Twitter.

27 March 2014

⇨ The above information is reprinted with kind permission from politics.co.uk.

How Chinese people bypass Tiananmen silence – online

Search for 'Tiananmen Square' on Chinese social media and you will usually draw a blank. But China's online community have adopted unconventional strategies to talk about the massacre 25 years ago.

You are unlikely to find anything under the search term 'Tiananmen Square' when trawling through China's biggest social networking site, despite it being 25 years since the massacre, writes freelance journalist Suswati Basu. In fact, any combination of numbers and words resembling 4 June 1989 has been blocked on China's Twitter-like site Weibo.

That is because the country's vast Internet censorship machine has been scrubbing clean any record of the event from social media sites down to its main search engine Baidu. Even on the 25th anniversary, the Communist party has continued its long-running campaign to force the Chinese public to forget the moment when People's Liberation Army soldiers opened fire on civilians in Beijing after months of protests in Tiananmen Square.

Consequently, all versions of Google and its services were blocked in the country today, in what was deemed as the most 'severe' crackdown during an anniversary, according to Internet censorship monitoring site greatfirewallofchina.org.

As seen in Baidu Baike, China's version of Google and Wikipedia, you will only find two entries for the year 1989: '1. 1989 is a leap year' and '2. 1989 is when Japan's Hesei era began'. However, despite the efforts of authorities employing the country's great firewall, comments made by Chinese Internet users over Tiananmen Square have remained intact in some places, even on Baidu's own Wiki page.

China's savvy netizens have taken to unconventional strategies in order to circumvent social media censors that are policing the social networking sites. They could be homophones (pronounced the same as a word likely to be censored but differs in meaning), euphemisms, characters that look almost the same (changing the typography) or words with English letters replacing the Chinese ones. It is a linguistic game of wits that takes place daily.

Since '4 June' would certainly have been blocked, one image that was shared last year was an edited version of the infamous 'tank man' that has become synonymous with the event. The satirical version comprised of Hong Kong's renowned giant rubber duck installation instead of tanks. The lone man blocking a column of tanks was also reimagined in Lego.

This year, the censors have also cracked down on images and symbols, including emoticons of candles to stop anyone from possibly showing sympathy to the hundreds of people who were killed. However, a recent poem that appeared online as an image said: 'Sail the ocean, sweep the square, clan king and eye field cannot be stopped!'

In Chinese, 'clan king' resembles the Chinese characters for 'democracy' with the exception of several strokes, while 'eye field' is typographically similar to the Chinese word for 'freedom'. Due to its mix of technologies, it was not detected and the poem managed to stay online.

There is no doubt that China's censors have gone beyond blocking expected sensitive terms like '25 years', but also blocking the code term 'May 35th' or the corresponding '535' code. Even the French-language 'six-quatre' and Roman numerals 'VIIIV' were blocked. Both 'square' and 'square dance' have also been blacklisted in this year's landmark anniversary.

Contrastingly on Twitter, the #TAM25 hashtag has seen a surge of users posting photographs of themselves with their faces covered and messages of support written on their hands.

And it is not just the world wide web authorities have been targeting. Chinese police have detained almost 60 people in the lead-up to 4 June. Amnesty International, which has been documenting the names of the activists held, said that China's President Xi Jinping was opting for 'repression over reform'. Amnesty General Secretary Salil Shetty added:

'The 25th Tiananmen anniversary was a critical test for President Xi's claims to be delivering greater openness (...) The response by the Chinese authorities to the 25th anniversary has been harsher than in previous years, as they persist with trying to wipe the events of 4 June from memory.'

Those detained in recent weeks include human rights lawyer Pu Zhiqiang and prominent journalist Gao Yu. Others, including Ding Zilin, spokesperson for the Tiananmen Mothers, have been placed under house arrest.

'It's not too late for Xi to change tack and we urge him to launch an open and independent investigation into the violent crackdown of 1989,' Shetty said.

4 June 2014

⇨ The above information is reprinted with kind permission from Channel 4. Please visit www.channel4.com/news for further information.

Internet repression in Vietnam continues as 30-month prison sentence for blogger is upheld

By Helen Clark

The 30-month prison sentence for Vietnamese human rights lawyer and blogger, Le Quoc Quan, was today upheld by a Hanoi appeals court. Quan, who has frequently blogged about human rights violations by the Government, was convicted in October 2013 on tax-evasion charges. He has been arbitrarily detained since December 2012. A crowd of hundreds wearing t-shirts in support of Quan were present outside the court, while a European Union delegation, representatives from the United States and Canada and a small group of journalists were present at the trial. This is just the latest move in the Vietnamese authorities' ongoing attack on dissent, free speech, free press and a free Internet.

If you need to communicate with someone the Vietnamese government is interested in keeping an eye, it is always been useful to be careful. Phone conversations can be listened to. Meetings at houses could be watched. Protests are invariably filmed by government operatives. If you were going to, say, chat via Gmail's chat function it should be switched to 'off the record' to prevent a copy of the discussion being archived. Some unlucky people have seen their blog posts traced to the Internet cafe they've later been arrested at. If you are a dissident you won't be the only one the police are interested in; they'll talk to your family, friends and employers, too. The latter they may ask to dismiss you.

It is Vietnam Ministry of Public Security conducts this surveillance work, while the Ministry of Information and Culture drafts many of the laws regarding Internet usage and 'abuse'. And it is most likely a unit within the MPS that is responsible for these, and earlier, malware attacks.

Much of the surveillance and intimidation is hardly new; similar operations took place during the Terror in the USSR. In fact, the CIA has compared the MPS with Russia's KGB. The KGB of comrade days, however, never had to deal with the vastness of the Internet. The government owns every newspaper and printing press in the country, but it has few serious servers, making control of the Internet difficult. It does not stop them from trying.

In January, the Associated Press in Vietnam reported on malware attacks against one of its journalists, against an American-Vietnamese blogger and against the Electronic Frontier Foundation (EFF). These are certainly not the first of their kind but may have been the first directed against those on foreign shores. The private correspondence of Vietnamese-American blogger Ngoc Tu was posted on her blog after someone – supposed, but not verified to be the Vietnamese government – sent her an email with a link that installed malware and key logging software giving the sender access to her password and her email account. The Associated Press reporter was a sent an email purportedly from Human Rights Watch with a link to a 'white paper' on human rights.

Vietnam's Internet history: enthusiasm and repression

Vietnam's relationship with the Internet has not been simple. The government has always been enthusiastic about the Internet and the wholesale benefits it could, and has, brought to the nation. Though classified as an 'enemy of the Internet' by Reporters Without Borders for its blocking of websites and arrests of bloggers and journalists, Vietnam's communist government has done an awful lot to ensure good Internet access.

But the country's vibrant Internet culture is a direct result of government guidance and intervention. Vietnam has long valued literacy and learning and according to Professor Carlyle Thayer at the Australian Defence Force Academy, the government believed that the 'knowledge era' was key to the nation's economic development. The Internet helped to provide that and greater world integration, something they have been increasingly keen for since Doi Moi in 1986 when the country began a period of economic renovation, shunning its former isolationist politics.

20 years ago the Vietnam Communist Party (CPV) noted three dangers facing the country: corruption, deviation from the socialist path and falling behind. The Internet was seen a perfect way to engage more with the world. A 2011 report by market research firm Cimigo, headquartered in Ho Chi Minh City, says: 'Vietnam has seen a more rapid growth of the Internet over the last few years than most other countries in the region and is one of the fastest growing Internet countries in the world… Since the year 2000, the number of Internet users in Vietnam has multiplied by about 120.'

However, the government misjudged, believing control to be easy, and circumventing its block beyond the ken of its citizens.

Putting the genie back in the bottle

There are three main laws bloggers, activists and others the state dislikes are charged under. Criminal Code Article 88 relates to 'conducting propaganda against the state'. This is the one most often used – both draconian and helpfully vague. Then there is Article 258, relating to 'abusing democratic freedoms', and Article 79 covering 'activities aimed overthrowing the Communist Party of Vietnam and People's Socialist Republic of Vietnam'.

However there have also been numerous Internet laws drafted, largely aimed at keeping citizens' net activities restricted to useful research or harmless entertainment. An August 2001 law imposed 'stringent' controls and required net cafe owners to report breaches to relevant authorities and to collect ID from their users. An August 2005 law criminalised using the Internet to oppose or destabilise the state, security, economy or social order, infringe on the rights of organisations or individuals, or mess around with Domain Name System (DNS) settings – something many Facebook users started doing in 2009. In October 2007 the Ministry of Information and Culture issued a decision requiring all businesses to obtain a licence before setting up a website. This has stymied growth in some ways, as it is only now that businesses are as present online as individuals.

In August 2008, Decree 97 made it illegal to 'abuse' the Internet to oppose the government. What got more attention was Circular 7, restricting bloggers to cover only personal, not political, topics. At the time blogging was a favoured pastime in Vietnam, Yahoo! 360 the favoured platform. Interest in blogging and blogs in general has since waned significantly. According to Cimigo, in 2009 40 per cent of Internet users visited blogs and 20 per cent blogged themselves. By 2011 those numbers had halved as people increasingly moved to social media sites like Facebook.

It was the quiet block of Facebook in 2009 that caught the world's attention. The government never mentioned a ban publicly though a purported scan of instructions to ISPs to block the site did rounds online. As the government never said much, Vietnam's legion of Facebook users simply muttered something about 'technical problems' as they 'fixed' the DNS settings to access the site.

What led to the Facebook block was the organising between previously disparate groups against Chinese-run bauxite mines in the Central Highlands of Vietnam – an already ecologically and politically sensitive area. Catholics, activists, environmentalists and anti-China activists all united via Facebook to protest the mines. In 2010 the government tried to launch its own social networking site (which led to headlines such as 'In Communist Vietnam, State Friends You'), go.vn, where users had to provide their full names and ID card details, but could also 'friend' communist luminaries. The Minister for Culture and Information Le Doan Hop praised the site's usefulness for young people and promotion of 'culture, values and benefits'.

In 2010, came a decision requiring all public hotels to install Green Dam monitoring software. Theoretically it allowed the government to see what was being looked at, possibly by whom and take appropriate steps. In fact decision 15/2010/QD-UBND was something of a paper tiger; many pointed out how such a piecemeal and scattershot approach would have limited utility and could be wholly circumvented by any serious activist, though rights organisations took the appropriate potshots as a matter of course.

In 2010, a ban was put in place, ostensibly on all online gaming between 10pm and 6am, to combat gaming addiction. However, it was never fully possible to enforce thanks to most popular games being hosted by overseas servers.

The most recent attempts at curbing net use via legislation has been Decree-Law 72 on Management of the Internet which formally came into effect in September 2013. Like many laws it is confusing and vague enough to be useful for any enthusiastic government prosecutor. Among other things it banned the sharing of news online. Or, rather, it banned the aggregation of news onto websites. The government took the time to publicly respond to the flurry of foreign concern and the head of the Ministry of Information and Culture's Online Information Section protested to Reuters that the law did not violate any of Vietnam's human rights commitments. 'We will never ban people from sharing information or linking news from websites,' he said, arguing it had been misinterpreted.

There has been talk that Decree 72 was also designed to protect intellectual property, as violations have long been problematic and go far beyond dollar copies of new Hollywood films on DVD. One of the things 72 supposedly sought to do was prevent websites re-posting news from its original source with no attribution and thus make things easier for news sites whilst also laying groundwork for membership of the Trans Pacific Partnership in regards to intellectual property protection.

The more interesting requirement was that ISPs locate servers, or at least one, within Vietnam and deliver information on users to the government, rather as Internet cafes have been required to do. They were also required to take down anything contravening laws. However Vietnam's most trafficked sites do not have servers within Vietnam and with such new laws do not entirely see the point, either. Indeed there are not many substantial servers located there at all, and bloggers who fear the law usually host their blogs overseas in any case. Should the government instruct local ISPs to block say, Google, many will simply respond again to 'technical difficulties' by readjusting their settings.

Peaceful evolution, draconian repression

The threat of peaceful and not so peaceful evolution hangs heavily over the heads of those in power in Hanoi.

Vietnam is regularly excoriated for its human rights record which generally means the way the nation locks up its dissidents, bloggers, religious leaders. Even US President Barack Obama made mention of blogger Dieu Cay's ongoing detention, ostensibly for tax reasons.

According to Human Rights Watch there were at least 63 political prisoners convicted in Vietnam last year. And yet, as Professor Thayer said in a 2011 paper: 'Great effort is put into monitoring, controlling and restricting Internet usage. The enormity of resources devoted for these purposes contrasts with the comparatively small number of political activists, religious leaders, and bloggers who have been arrested, tried and sentenced to prison.'

Though the numbers have increased since the above was written there is still little mass organising in this area, and large-scale protests tend to be over more concrete issues: workers' rights and wages or land grabs. However, those considered potentially subversive are closely monitored, watched by both a physical presence and an online one.

Actual harassment of bloggers and their families has been common over the years. Most famously, mother of Vietnamese blogger Ta Phong Tan set herself on fire outside the Bac Lieu People's Committee building in the Mekong Delta in July 2012, in protest at the way her daughter had been treated.

Within the MPS are units that monitor all forms of communication and there are records of the country purchasing more complicated surveillance equipment. According to the same 2011 paper by Professor Thayer, Vietnam by 2002 had the Verint call monitoring system. Verint, a US company, supplies over 150 nations and 10,000 organisations with varied forms of security and monitoring equipment.

China in the 1990s also offered technical assistance to 'monitor internal threats to national security' to the General Department II. The military also collects intelligence related to national security and with attention paid to those, abroad or within Vietnam, who 'plot or engage in activities aimed at threatening or opposing the Communist Party of Vietnam or the Socialist Republic of Vietnam'.

General Department II not only, arguably, watched dissidents but also tapped senior party officials in an incident of usually opaque factionalism that later came to light.

There have been many attacks against varied blogs and websites; 16 starting in 2009 and intensifying in April of the next year. Varied activists came under fire: Catholics discussing land issues – there have been ongoing spats between Catholics and the state over land grabs – as well as environmentalists and political agitators. Sites allied to the anti-bauxite movement were also hit. IP addresses were allegedly traced back to within Vietnam and to addresses connected to the military. The attacks, verified by McAfee and Google, were botnet attacks where spyware hid in seemingly innocuous Vietnamese language keystroke software (though a Romanised alphabet Vietnamese has 29 letters and many diacritics). Neel Mehta, a security expert with Google, wrote in a blog post that: 'While the malware itself was not especially sophisticated, it has nonetheless been used for damaging purposes.'

Vietnam joining the 'technology race'?

That Vietnam has taken up the Internet quickly and with great passion is beyond dispute but there are still gaps in the industry. Everyone may be using Google but few local businesses are profiting from the web and mobile boom.

Bryan Pelz, an IT developer, says there is 'no means for direct monetization'.

'The banking industry and regulatory environment hasn't taken strong steps to lay the groundwork for easy online payments. Essentially nobody has credit cards. If you're building a website and hope to charge users or make a living off of advertising, it's a tough road in Vietnam.'

And despite talented hackers and software engineers – Flappy Bird was designed by a Vietnamese engineer – with experience and skill comparable to the rest of Asia, software isn't considered a hugely lucrative field, according to Pelz.

Of those aged 15–24, according to Cimigo, 95 per cent are online and spend over two hours each day on the web, via Internet cafe, desktop or phone. 95 per cent use it for news. Google remains the top-rated site in Vietnam, followed by local entertainment hub Zing. News sites Dan Tri and Tuoi Tre also feature, as does Yahoo!, Facebook and YouTube.

Last year a Russian-backed challenger to Google called Coc Coc (knock knock) opened shop. It has aimed to take some of Google's 97 per cent market share, the reasoning being that Google had no offices in Vietnam and did not have algorithms well written enough to understand Vietnamese well. Unlike other startups it was backed with serious investment and a staff of over 300, according to the AP.

A recent article in *The Atlantic* reported that Vietnam's Ministry of Science and Technology has sponsored something called the Silicon Valley Project which aims to push Vietnam to be more than a simple producer of electronic parts (Intel has a one billion USD plant in the country) to a tech powerhouse with a strong startup industry and innovative firms. The recent success of Flappy Bird – one of the most downloaded apps ever – is seen as evidence of Vietnam's larger potential.

Indeed the Silicon Valley Project's mission statement is not dissimilar to the Communist Party's mid-1990s, ideas about the upcoming 'knowledge era': 'This is the time for Vietnam to join in the technology race. Countries which fail to change with this technology-driven world will fall into a vicious cycle of backwardness and poverty.'

This government-backed and sanctioned creativity and entrepreneurship has been lauded, though it's also been pointed out how it may rather clash with many of the Internet restrictions set out in varied laws, such as Decree 72. Of course Vietnam's ministries do not always march in-sync and what the Ministry of Information and Culture believes to be good may clash with a more pro-tech Ministry of Science and Technology.

The confirmation today that Le Quoc Quan is facing 30 months behind bars, does not bode well for the future of Internet freedom in Vietnam.

20 February 2014

⇨ The above information is reprinted with kind permission from Index on Censorship. Please visit www.indexoncensorship.org for further information.

Freedom of the press 2014: media freedom hits decade low

Global press freedom has fallen to its lowest level in over a decade, according to a Freedom House report released today. The decline was driven in part by major regression in several Middle Eastern states, including Egypt, Libya and Jordan; marked setbacks in Turkey, Ukraine and a number of countries in East Africa; and deterioration in the relatively open media environment of the United States.

Freedom of the Press 2014 found that despite positive developments in a number of countries, most notably in sub-Saharan Africa, setbacks were the dominant trend in every other region. The share of the world's population with media rated 'Free' remains at just 14 percent, or only one in seven people. Far larger shares live in 'Not Free' (44 per cent) or 'Partly Free' (42 per cent) media environments.

'We see declines in media freedom on a global level, driven by governments' efforts to control the message and punish the messenger,' said Karin Karlekar, project director of the report. 'In every region of the world last year, we found both governments and private actors attacking reporters, blocking their physical access to newsworthy events, censoring content, and ordering politically motivated firings of journalists.'

'In 2013 we saw more cases of states targeting foreign reporters and media outlets,' Karlekar added. 'Russian and Chinese authorities declined to renew or threatened to withhold visas for prominent foreign correspondents, but the new

Egyptian government went a step further by detaining a number of Al-Jazeera staff on charges of supporting terrorism.'

Key global findings:

Of the 197 countries and territories assessed during 2013, a total of 63 (32 per cent) were rated Free, 68 (35 per cent) were rated Partly Free, and 66 (33 per cent) were rated Not Free.

All regions except sub-Saharan Africa, whose average score levelled off, showed declines, with the Middle East and North Africa suffering the worst deterioration.

Triggers for country declines included governments' overt attempts to control the news – whether through the physical harassment of journalists covering protest movements or other sensitive stories, restrictions on foreign reporters, or tightened constraints on online news outlets and social media – as well as the role of owners in shaping media content through directives on coverage or dismissals of outspoken journalists.

Country improvements were largely driven by three factors: a growing ability of private firms to operate television and radio outlets; greater access to a variety of views via online media, social media and international outlets;

and improved respect for legal protections for the press.

China and Russia maintained a tight grip on local media while also attempting to control the more independent views provided either in the blogosphere or by foreign news sources.

The world's eight worst-rated countries remain Belarus, Cuba, Equatorial Guinea, Eritrea, Iran, North Korea, Turkmenistan and Uzbekistan.

Key egional findings:

Americas:

The regional average score worsened to its lowest level in five years, and just two per cent of the population in Latin America lived in Free media environments.

Scores dropped in Honduras, Panama, Suriname and Venezuela.

Paraguay's rating improved to Partly Free.

Conditions in the United States deteriorated due primarily to attempts by the government to inhibit reporting on national security issues.

Asia-Pacific:

Only five per cent of the region's population had access to Free media in 2013.

China, rated Not Free, continued to crack down on online speech, particularly on microblogs, and also ramped up pressure on foreign journalists.

Press freedom deteriorated in Hong Kong, India, Sri Lanka, Thailand, and several Pacific Island states, including Nauru, which was downgraded to Partly Free.

Burma and Nepal registered score improvements.

Eurasia:

The overwhelming majority of people in the region (97 per cent) lived in Not Free media environments.

Conditions in Russia remained grim, as the RIA Novosti news agency was closed and the government enacted additional legal restrictions on online speech.

Ukraine was downgraded to Not Free for 2013 due primarily to attacks on journalists covering the Euromaidan protests, and further erosion took place in Azerbaijan.

Positive developments occurred in Kyrgyzstan and Georgia.

Europe:

This region enjoys the highest level of press freedom, but the regional average score registered the second-largest drop worldwide in 2013.

The Netherlands, Norway and Sweden were rated the world's top-performing countries.

Significant decline took place in Turkey, which fell into the Not Free category, as well as in Greece, Montenegro and the United Kingdom.

A modest numerical improvement was noted in Italy, which remains Partly Free.

Middle East and North Africa:

Only two per cent of the region's people lived in Free media environments, while the vast majority, 84 per cent, lived in Not Free countries or territories.

Backsliding occurred in Libya, which fell back into the Not Free category, and Egypt, where the military-led government limited press freedom.

Significant deterioration took place in Jordan and to a lesser extent in Iraq and the United Arab Emirates. Press freedom declined further in Syria, in the midst of an especially brutal civil war that posed enormous dangers to journalists.

Improvements took place in Algeria (upgraded to Partly Free), Yemen, the West Bank and Gaza Strip, and Israel (upgraded back to Free).

Sub-Saharan Africa:

The majority of people (56 per cent) lived in countries with Partly Free media. Improvements in the legal and economic spheres in 2013 were balanced by declines in the political category.

Declines occurred in South Sudan and Zambia (both downgraded to Not Free), the Central African Republic, and several countries in East Africa, including Kenya, Mozambique, Tanzania, and Uganda.

West Africa saw a number of improvements, including the upgrade of Côte d'Ivoire to Partly Free and numerical gains in Mali, Senegal, and Togo.

Other gains were recorded in the Democratic Republic of Congo, Madagascar, the Seychelles, and Zimbabwe.

1 May 2014

⇨ The above information is reprinted with kind permission from Freedom House. Please visit www.freedomhouse.org for further information.

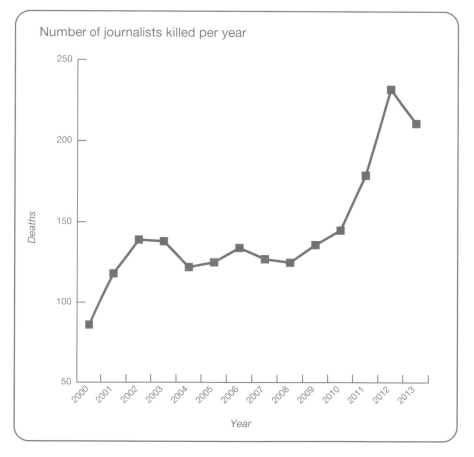

Number of journalists killed per year

Cameron warns UK press: sign up to royal charter or else

PM says UK press risks 'hideous statutory regulation' in future if it declines to seek recognition under terms of new royal charter.

By Nicholas Watt

David Cameron has warned the press that it runs the risk of facing 'hideous statutory regulation' in the future if the Independent Press Standards Organisation declines to seek recognition under the terms of the new royal charter.

In an interview with *The Spectator*'s editor, Fraser Nelson, a strong campaigner against the royal charter, Cameron said a 'less liberal, less enlightened government' of the future could impose statutory controls unless the press acted now.

The Prime Minister spoke out a few weeks after 90% of national newspapers and most regional publishers announced that they would join the Independent Press Standards Organisation (Ipso). The body, whose members include the Telegraph Media Group, Associated Newspapers, News UK, Trinity Mirror and Northern & Shell, is declining to seek recognition from a panel that is to be established under the terms of the royal charter.

Ipso believes the recognition panel, to be set up by the former Permanent Secretary at the Home Office, Sir David Normington, who is now commissioner for public appointments, amounts to an unacceptable level of state control. Cameron, who agreed the terms of the royal charter with Labour and the Liberal Democrats, says the new system places the Government at arm's length from the body.

The royal charter can only be amended by a two-thirds majority vote in both Houses of Parliament. The recognition panel will not regulate the press but will assess every few years whether a regulatory body, which signs up, is carrying out its functions in line with the principles laid down in Lord Justice Leveson's report into the press. Once a regulatory body is recognised by the panel, section 40 of the Crime and Courts Act 2013 would

be triggered meaning that publishers outside an officially recognised regulatory body could suffer financial penalties in legal actions.

Cameron told *The Spectator*: 'I believe there's a great opportunity here to put this difficult and painful issue to bed. If the press set up their regulator I hope, in time, they will make that regulator compliant with – will be able to then seek recognition under – the charter recognition body.

'If that then happens, we'll have in place a system that I think will settle this issue because we would have achieved what Leveson wanted which is independent self-regulation by the press, but not marking its own homework, having itself checked, and only having the body checked as it were by the charter.'

The Prime Minister denied he was adopting a tougher stance than Maria Miller, the Culture Secretary, who suggested on *The Andrew Marr Show* on BBC1 recently that nothing else needed to happen if Ipso was seen to work. Cameron told *The Spectator*: 'What she's saying is that it's now down to the press. We've done our bit, we have put in place a royal charter. We've given you, the press, an opportunity to put this issue to bed I would think for 50 to 100 years if you want to.

'Now, if you choose to set up your self-regulator but say "we're not going to seek recognition", that is your choice. Personally I think that is a mistake because you're missing the opportunity to settle this and you're risking that some future, less liberal, less enlightened government at the time of the next press crisis will hitch you with some hideous statutory regulation which I prevented.'

The Prime Minister told Nelson the press could walk away from the recognition panel if it felt a government was restricting freedom

of expression. He told *The Spectator* editor: 'If ever that happens, the press can say: "We're no longer seeking recognition."'It is a voluntary system.'

But Cameron was criticised for warning of tighter regulation if the new body declines to seek recognition from the panel. Kirsty Hughes, chief executive of Index on Censorship, said: 'David Cameron should be looking at why his royal charter is damaging to press freedom. This is a point of fundamental principle and the press should stick to their guns. You don't walk away from a fundamental principle just because someone threatens that it could get even worse.'

Douglas Carswell, the Conservative MP for Harwich, said: 'I think this proposed royal charter is indefensible and it's bang out of order to try to defend it on the basis that a future government might do something even more indefensible. The press in this country hasn't been forced to publish under licence for centuries and it would be a massive black mark against this government if they push ahead with this folly.'

The Spectator declined to print Cameron's remarks in the Christmas edition of the magazine, which ran a lengthy interview with the Prime Minister. Nelson instead blogged his comments on the press early on Boxing Day.

The Guardian and *The Observer* have reserved judgment on whether to join Ipso.

26 December 2013

⇨ The above information is reprinted with kind permission from *The Guardian*. Please visit www.theguardian.com for further information.

UK Press Freedom Report

Global press organisation releases report from January mission; British Government 'must take steps to ensure it upholds the high standards of press freedom expected from a leading democracy.'

The World Association of Newspapers and News Publishers (WAN-IFRA) today releases the results from a fact-finding delegation of international editors sent to the United Kingdom between 15 and 16 January 2014.

'The lack of any real guarantees enshrining press freedom continues to expose journalism in the United Kingdom to great uncertainty, as there is nothing benign in a system that invites even the possibility of tighter restrictions on freedom of expression,' said WAN-IFRA CEO, Vincent Peyrègne.

'If the UK Government feels it is acceptable, in the name of national security, to dictate what is in the public interest, and given the UK's continued influence over developing nations where media are essential for the spread of democratic values, the future of a free, independent press that can hold power to account is under threat worldwide.'

The WAN-IFRA delegation met government representatives, industry professionals, academics, lawyers and civil society organisations and heard a range of opinions regarding proposed changes to the system of self-regulation and the acrimonious process surrounding the drawing up of the royal charter.

The report reiterates serious industry concerns regarding the reforms, while revealing cautious optimism from those who believe current proposals to be an opportunity to restore public trust following Lord Justice Leveson's Inquiry into press standards.

The report also details UK Government interference in the editorial independence of *The Guardian* newspaper, calling for stronger support for public interest journalism. The intense pressure applied by UK authorities following publication of digital surveillance stories based on leaked information from NSA whistle-blower, Edward Snowden, provoked a high level of international solidarity with *The Guardian*'s position from within the WAN-IFRA membership.

The report findings also call for:

⇨ The British Government to reiterate clearly to the international community that it continues to support a free and independent press.

⇨ Foreign governments not to transpose like-for-like the British model of regulation, calling for internationally recognised standards of freedom of expression to be applied to specific national contexts.

⇨ Any regulatory system of the press to have the support of the industry, and for reform discussions to be transparent and open to public consultation.

⇨ The highest standards of professionalism and ethical practice at every level of the media industry.

16 January 2014

⇨ The above information is reprinted with kind permission from the World Association of Newspapers and News Publishers. Please visit www.wan-ifra.org for further information.

World Press Freedom Index 2014

Biggest rises and falls in the 2014 World Press Freedom Index.

The 2014 *World Press Freedom Index* spotlights the negative impact of conflicts on freedom of information and its protagonists. The ranking of some countries has also been affected by a tendency to interpret national security needs in an overly broad and abusive manner to the detriment of the right to inform and be informed. This trend constitutes a growing threat worldwide and is even endangering freedom of information in countries regarded as democracies. Finland tops the index for the fourth year running, closely followed by The Netherlands and Norway, like last year. At the other end of the index, the last three positions are again held by Turkmenistan, North Korea and Eritrea, three countries where freedom of information is non-existent. Despite occasional turbulence in the past year, these countries continue to be news and information black holes and living hells for the journalists who inhabit them. This year's index covers 180 countries, one more than last year. The new entry, Belize, has been assigned an enviable position (29th). Cases of violence against journalists are rare in Belize but there were some problems: defamation suits involving demands for large amounts in damages, national security restrictions on implementation of the Freedom of Information Act and sometimes unfair management of broadcast frequencies.

Falls due to armed conflicts

The 2014 index underscores the negative correlation between freedom of information and conflicts, both open conflicts and undeclared ones. In an unstable environment, the media become strategic goals and targets for groups or individuals whose attempts to control news and information violate the guarantees enshrined in international law, in particular, Article 19 of the International Covenant on Civil and Political Rights, the 1949 Geneva Conventions and the 1977 Protocols Additional 1 and 2 to the Geneva Conventions.

Syria (unchanged at 177th) has been an extreme example of this since March 2011. Now one of the countries where freedom of information and its actors are most in danger, it rubs shoulders with the bottom three. The Syrian crisis has also had dramatic repercussions throughout the region, reinforcing media polarization in Lebanon (106th, -4), encouraging the Jordanian authorities to tighten their grip, and accelerating the spiral of violence in Iraq (153rd, -2), where tension between Shiites and Sunnis is growing.

In Iran (173rd, +2), one of the Middle East's key countries, there has so far been no implementation of the promises to improve freedom of information that the new President, Hassan Rouhani, made. Coverage of the Syrian tragedy in both the official Iranian press and on the blogosphere is closely watched by the regime, which cracks down on any criticism of its foreign policy.

This negative correlation is also seen in the big falls registered by Mali (122nd, -22) and Central African Republic (109th, -34). The open or internecine warfare destabilizing Democratic Republic of Congo (151st, -8) and the activities of guerrillas and terrorist groups in Somalia (176th, unchanged) and Nigeria (112th, +4) prevented any significant improvement in their ranking.

The formation of a government led by Mohamed Morsi in Egypt (159th, unchanged) in the summer 2012 was accompanied by an increase in abuses against journalists and all-out efforts to bring the media under the Muslim Brotherhood's control. That was brought to a complete halt by the army's return to power a year later. The ensuing persecution of the Muslim Brotherhood affected not only Egyptian journalists but also their Turkish, Palestinian and Syrian colleagues. In the Persian Gulf, especially the United Arab Emirates (118th, -3), bloggers and journalists were arrested and tried on charges of links to the Brotherhood.

The upsurge in violence against journalists finally elicited a response from the international community – in terms of resolutions, at least. The United Nations General Assembly adopted its first-ever resolution on the safety of journalists by consensus on 26 November. It included a call for 2 November to be celebrated as International Day to End Impunity for crimes of violence against journalists.

It was unquestionably a step in the right direction, complementing Resolution 1738 condemning attacks on journalists in armed conflicts, which the Security Council adopted in December 2006 on Reporters Without Borders' initiative, and the UN Plan of Action on the Safety of Journalists and Impunity, adopted in April 2012. Reporters Without Borders now wants the UN to create a group of independent experts with the task of monitoring respect by member states for their obligations; in particular, their obligation to protect journalists, to investigate all cases of violence against them, and bring those responsible to justice.

Information sacrificed to national security and surveillance

Countries that pride themselves on being democracies and respecting the rule of law have not set an example, far from it. Freedom of information is too often sacrificed to an overly broad and abusive interpretation of national security needs, marking a disturbing retreat from democratic practices. Investigative journalism often suffers as a result.

This has been the case in the United States (46th), which fell 13 places, one of the most significant declines, amid increased efforts to track down whistleblowers and the sources of leaks. The trial and conviction of Private Bradley Manning and the pursuit of NSA analyst Edward Snowden were warnings to all those thinking of assisting in the disclosure of sensitive information that would clearly be in the public interest.

US journalists were stunned by the Department of Justice's seizure of Associated Press phone records without warning in order to identify the source of a CIA leak. It served as a reminder of the urgent need for a 'shield law' to protect the confidentiality of journalists' sources at the federal level. The revival of the legislative process is little consolation for James Risen of *The New York Times*, who is subject to a court order to testify against a former CIA employee accused of leaking classified information. And less still for Barrett Brown, a young freelance journalist facing 105 years in prison in connection with the posting of information that hackers obtained from Statfor, a private intelligence company with close ties to the federal government.

The United Kingdom (33rd, -3) distinguished itself in the war on terror by the disgraceful pressure it put on *The Guardian* newspaper and by its detention of David Miranda, journalist Glenn Greenwald's partner and assistant, for nine hours. Both the US and UK authorities seem obsessed with hunting down whistleblowers instead of adopting legislation to rein in abusive surveillance practices that negate privacy, a democratic value cherished in both countries.

The 'special intelligence protection bill' that the National Diet in Japan (59th, – 5) adopted in late 2013 would reduce government transparency on such key national issues as nuclear power and relations with the United States, now enshrined as taboos. Investigative journalism, public interest and the confidentiality of journalists' sources are all being sacrificed by legislators bent on ensuring that their country's image is spared embarrassing revelations.

The 'war on terror' is also being exploited by governments that are quick to treat journalists as 'threats to national security'. Dozens of journalists have been jailed on this pretext in Turkey (154th), especially for covering the Kurdish issue. In Morocco, unchanged in 136th position, the authorities readily confused journalism with terrorism since the case of online newspaper editor Ali Anouzla. In Israel (96th, +17), freedom of information is often sacrificed to purported security requirements.

In India's northern Kashmir region, mobile Internet and communications are suspended in response to any unrest. In the north of Sri Lanka (165th, -2), the army reigns supreme, tolerating no challenge to the official vision of the 'pacification' process in Tamil separatism's former strongholds. Alarmed by the Arab Spring turmoil, authoritarian regimes in the Arabian Peninsula and Central Asia have

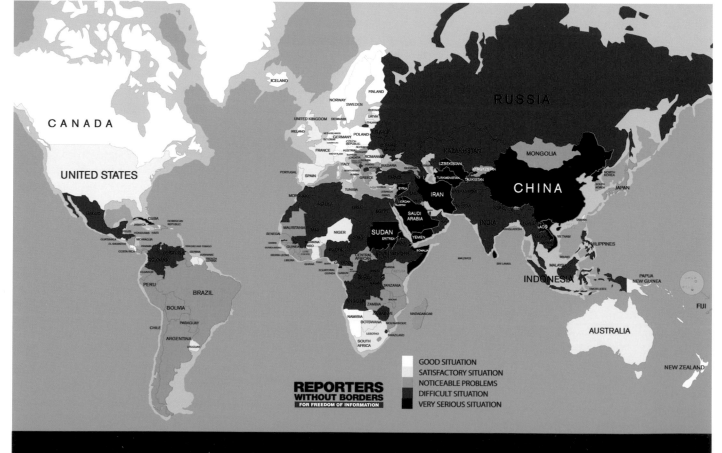

FREEDOM OF THE PRESS WORLDWIDE IN 2014

stepped up media censorship and surveillance to head off any 'attempt at destabilization'.

Privatisation of violence

Non-state groups constitute the main source of physical danger for journalists in a number of countries. The militias fomenting chaos in the new Libya (137th, -5) and Yemeni armed groups linked to Al-Qaeda in the Arabian Peninsula are leading examples of this privatization of violence. Al-Shabaab in Somalia (176th, unchanged) and the M23 movement in Democratic Republic of Congo (151st, -8) both regard journalists as enemies. Jihadi groups such as Jabhat Al-Nosra and Islamic State in Iraq and the Levant (ISIS) use violence against news providers as part of their drive to control the regions they 'liberate.'

Organized crime is a fearsome predator for journalists in many parts of the world, especially Honduras (129th, -1), Guatemala (125th, -29), Brazil (111th, -2) and Paraguay (105th, -13), but also Pakistan, China, Kyrgyzstan and the Balkans. In organized crime's shadow, it is hard if not impossible to refrain from self-censorship on such sensitive subjects as drug-trafficking, corruption and criminal penetration of the state apparatus. The passivity or indifference often shown by authorities towards crimes of violence against the media, or sometimes even their connivance or direct involvement, reinforces the impunity enjoyed by those responsible and fuels the cycle of violence against news providers.

The indicator is a tool for measuring overall performance. The breakdown of the indicator's scores by region shows a worsening in all continents except Asia, where it was unchanged. Like last year, the European Union and Balkans obtained the best score (17.6), followed by the Americas (30.3), Africa (35.6), Asia-Pacific (42.2), Eastern Europe and Central Asia (45.5) and finally Middle East and North Africa (48.7).

Annual media freedom indicator: 3456 in 2014 (3,395 in 2013)

⇨ European Union and Balkans: 17.6 (17.5)

⇨ Americas: 30.3 (30.0)

⇨ Africa : 35.6 (34.3)

⇨ Asia-Pacific: 42.2 (42.2)

⇨ Eastern Europe and Central Asia: 45.5 (45.3)

⇨ Middle East and North Africa: 48.7 (48.5)

Noteworthy falls

In the Americas, the 13-place fall registered by the United States (46th, -13) was more than doubled by Guatemala (125th, -29), which saw a two-fold increase in the number of physical attacks on journalists, including four murders, and was equalled by Paraguay (105th, -13), where the pressure on journalists to censor themselves keeps on mounting. Paraguay had already plummeted last year, following a coup in June 2012, three years after a coup sent Honduras (129th, -1) to the level where it remains in the current post-election chaos.

In Africa, the two most noteworthy falls, by Mali and Central African Republic, were due to armed conflicts mentioned above. In Burundi, where a presidential election is imminent, the senate passed a law restricting the freedom of journalists. In Kenya (90th, -18), the government's much criticized authoritarian response to the media's coverage of the Westgate Mall attacks was compounded by dangerous parliamentary initiatives, above all a law adopted at the end of 2013 creating a special court to judge audiovisual content.

In Guinea (102nd, -15), journalists found it dangerous and difficult to work during elections marked by many protests. Several journalists were attacked or injured by over-excited demonstrators or by members of the security forces dispersing the protests. Zambia (93rd, -20), which had progressed in recent years, was dragged down by measures to censor and block news websites. Finally, rulers who have clung to power for years and fear change got tougher with the media, resulting in abusive prosecutions in Chad (139th, -17) and several closures in Cameroon (131st, -10).

The 13-place fall by Kuwait (91st) reflects the somewhat tougher line pursued by the authorities. A draconian bill was proposed and then abandoned in the spring of 2013. It would have allowed the authorities to fine journalists up to 300,000 dinars (one million dollars) for criticizing the Emir or the Crown Prince, or misrepresenting what they say, and impose sentences of up to ten years in prison on journalists who insult God, the Prophets of Islam, or the Prophet Mohamed's wives or companions.

These spectacular changes should not make us forget the tragic immobility at the bottom of the index where Vietnam (173rd, -1), Uzbekistan (166th, -1) and Saudi Arabia (164th, unchanged), to name but three, continue to tighten their grip on news and information and adapt their methods of radical censorship to the digital era. The cruellest punishments await those of their citizens who have the courage to resist. In Kazakhstan (161st, unchanged) and Azerbaijan (160th, -3), media pluralism is in the process of succumbing to the increasingly repressive tendencies of rulers clinging to power.

Noteworthy rises

Violence against journalists, direct censorship and misuse of judicial proceedings are on the decline in Panama (87th, +25), Dominican Republic (68th, +13), Bolivia (94th, +16) and Ecuador (94th, +25), although in Ecuador the level of media polarisation is still high and often detrimental to public debate.

The past year was marked by laudable legislative developments in some countries such as South Africa (42nd, +11), where the President refused to sign a law that would have endangered investigative journalism.

In Georgia (84th, +17), the 2013 presidential election was less tense that the previous year's parliamentary elections, which were marked by physical attacks and hate campaigns against journalists. Thanks to political cohabitation and then a change of government through the polls, Georgia has recovered some of the terrain lost in recent years as the Saakashvili administration's reforming zeal ran out of steam. Media polarization will nonetheless continue to be a challenge in the coming years.

Israel's 17-place rise must be offset against its 20-place fall in the 2013 index as a result of Operation *Pillar of Defense* in November 2012, when two Palestinian journalists were killed, and the many raids it carried out against Palestinian media. Security needs continue to be used as an excuse to limit freedom of information. The Israeli media are able to be outspoken but media located in 'Israeli territory' must comply with prior military censorship and gag orders. Investigative reporting involving national security is not welcome.

Abusive treatment of Palestinian and foreign journalists by the Israel Defence Forces is common, especially during the weekly demonstrations at the Separation Wall. Many photojournalists were deliberately targetted when leaving the demonstrations in November 2013. On 4 December, an Israeli high court endorsed the seizure of equipment from Wattan TV during an IDF raid in February 2012.

Timor-Leste (77th) rose 14 places in the wake of a historic journalists' congress in Dili on 25–27 October at which a code of professional conduct and the creation of a seven-member Press Council were approved. But continuing vigilance is needed. The media law currently before Parliament is the next challenge for media freedom in Timor-Leste.

31 January 2014

⇨ The above information is reprinted with kind permission from Reporters Without Borders. Please visit www.rsf. org for further information.

Hamas censors British journalists. Why don't we care?

By Douglas Murray

I wonder if any readers have an answer to this question: has anybody, throughout this whole conflict around Gaza, heard any reporter inside Gaza, at any time, preface or conclude their remarks with 'reporting from Gaza, under Hamas government reporting restrictions'? I don't watch television news all the time and so may have missed it, but I don't think I have heard this said even once.

Which is strange. When reporting from a dictatorship like Gaza it used to be the norm that reporters would preface or conclude any report with some variant of this formula. Doing so was a neat way to send the warning to viewers that you were reporting from a place where the authorities were censoring what you could say.

Before the 2003 war in Iraq, for instance, reporters broadcasting for television or radio from inside Iraq nearly always made reference to the fact that they were reporting under restrictions imposed on them by Saddam Hussein's government. This often meant a Hussein goon was standing nearby checking that nothing untoward was said.

In the same way, Hamas takes great care to ensure that the 'wrong'

message does not come out. Indeed they recently expelled a reporter from the Putin propaganda channel Russia Today because he mentioned that Hamas were launching rockets from Gaza.

Yet I can think of no example during this conflict when reporters for any major broadcaster have told the truth – which is that if they stay in Gaza they are only able to tell Hamas's account of this conflict (complete with 'deliberate' Israeli targeting and only ever 'innocent', never 'guilty' victims). There will be those who think this a small technical point. But I suspect this is one major reason why some surprising Western observers seem to have become so rancidly pro-Hamas during this conflict.

3 August 2014

⇨ The above information is reprinted with kind permission from *The Spectator*. Please visit blogs.spectator.co.uk for further information.

China censorship: journalists strike at *Southern Weekend* over censorship in New Year editorial

By Jessica Elgot

Journalists at one of China's most influential papers have stunned the country by going on strike over censorship of their paper's New Year message, which was changed by propaganda officials.

Southern Weekend staff have demanded that the Guangdong censorship officials resign over the changing of the editorial message, which called for political change.

Student protesters joined the demonstrations by the journalists, who held banners calling for 'press freedom, constitutionalism and democracy'.

Southern Weekend, unlikely much state-run media like the Xinhua news agency or broadcaster CCTV, is known for investigative journalism, testing the limits of free speech in the nation.

The New Year editorial, which called for the cementing of rights into a constitution, entitled 'Dream of China, Dream of Constitutionalism' was changed to gushing praise of the Chinese Communist Party.

'Dream of China' is a favoured saying of new Chinese premier Xi Jinping.

Some of the protesters carried banners that read: 'We want press freedom, constitutionalism and democracy'.

In two open letters 35 prominent former staff and 50 interns at the paper demanded the provincial head of propaganda Tuo Zhen immediately resign for his interference, which they say overstepped his duties.

The first open letter, translated by China Media Project, said: 'We are just a group of young people with ideals, even as "ideals" at present meet with mockery. Essentially, these ideals are the hope that their own country can be better, the hope that their own people can live happily.

'This newspaper has for many years been a paper that sincerely loves its country and its people. The people [who work] there hope, in a spirit of good-will, that their country can be better.

'How can a country determined to become a culturally strong nation employ methods lacking culture to manage culture?

'How can a country that is building its international image permit people to use rude and arbitrary methods that damage the country's reputation?'

A statement from *Southern Weekly* via Weibo, released on Sunday, said in 2012 1,034 news reports were revised or cancelled due to censorship.

But more outrage was ignited when the newspaper's official microblogging profile sent out a number of tweets denying the change was caused by censorship officials, and had in fact been approved by senior editors.

China News Network, a popular blog run by journalism students in China and abroad, said editors and reporters had tweeted on Sino Weibo, China's Twitter equivalent, that they had been forced to hand over their passwords to the microblogging sites, to state officials.

Southern Weekend journalist and head of its social media operations Wu Wei confirmed that he was forced to hand over his password for the paper's account on Sina Weibo.

Another message appeared on the Weibo account of the paper's business desk, saying the paper's social media operations had been seized by propaganda officials.

More than 100 reporters signed a letter, saying the Weibo statement where the newspaper took responsibility for the editorial changes, was a fake, reported the Hong Kong-based *South China Morning Post*.

'The statement [on the official microblog] does not represent the opinion of the editorial staff. It is a result of pressure applied by the authorities.

'The editorial staff will fight against the falsified statement. Until the issue is resolved, we will not do any editorial work.'

Reporters and editors told China News Network that since the appointment of Tuo in May 2012, they are now required to submit their news topics to censors before they even begin reporting.

One reporter, who remains anonymous, told China News Network her stories had been 'raped'.

Searches for 'Southern Weekend' have now been blocked on Weibo, returning a message that reads: 'According to relevant laws, regulations and policies the search results for "Southern Weekly" cannot be shown.'

Students, journalists and social media protesters are now calling for supporters to 'occupy' locations in Beijing, Shanghai and Guangdong.

7 January 2013

⇨ The above information is reprinted with kind permission from The Huffington Post UK. Please visit www.huffingtonpost.co.uk for further information.

How a film or DVD is rated

The BBFC's age ratings decisions are reached by consensus, with the Director, the President and the two Vice-Presidents taking ultimate responsibility.

The Examiners' daily viewing programme consists of a combination of film and DVD material. Until July 2012, some Examiners also specialised in video games, as rating an interactive game could be a very different experience to rating a film or DVD.

Examiners normally view DVD submissions on their own – called solo viewing. A large proportion of works suitable for solo viewing include episodes from TV series or works aimed at young children that have already been broadcast on television. Films for cinema release are rated in teams of two. Controversial works, such as extreme reality material, will also be programmed for team work and often seen by more than one team

in order to gather diverse opinions.

Examiners watch films for cinema release in the BBFC's cinema, in order to accurately reproduce the effect that sound levels and special effects will have on the cinema audience. DVDs are viewed in the BBFC's viewing rooms on plasma screens, to recreate the 'home viewing' experience.

Many films and DVDs are submitted in foreign languages (notably Hindi and other South Asian languages) and Examiners with linguistic skills are programmed to view these works. Where the work is in a language not spoken by any of the Examiners and there are no subtitles, the BBFC will use an interpreter who will sit alongside the Examiner or team.

With each work, Examiners log details of what they watch, including:

⇨ general context – plot, characters, outline of individual scenes

⇨ timings of key moments, including camera angles, type of shots, on- and off-screen moments

⇨ bad language, sex and drug references and so on.

Reports include a brief synopsis of the work, details of the issues and an argument in support of the recommended age rating. Most decisions are straightforward and are based on the BBFC's published Guidelines, which were last revised in 2009. The distributor can request a specific age

rating, which the solo Examiner or team will take into consideration, but such a request does not determine the final decision. If necessary and appropriate, cuts may be suggested to meet the category request, and the decision will be ultimately made by the distributor.

A work is referred for further viewing by a team if an Examiner is unsure about an issue or theme.

Sometimes a work will fall between two categories. This second team could include a Senior Examiner or an Examiner with expertise in the particular subject, as well as the Director and the Head of Policy.

Difficult or controversial material can also be referred to the weekly Examiners' Meeting, where they can be debated further to obtain a wide range of valuable opinions. Ultimately, the work will be referred to Senior Management.

If a work contains material which is illegal or unacceptable under the BBFC's Guidelines, Examiners will draw up a list of cuts which will be sent to the distributor. If a work as a whole is unacceptable, it can be rejected, but this happens only on rare occasions. The Presidential Team will be consulted on difficult works, especially those which may be refused a certificate altogether or which raise serious policy issues.

⇨ The above information is reprinted with kind permission from the BBFC. Please visit www.bbfc. co.uk for further information.

© BBFC 2014

Film censorship in the UK: a brief history

Film4.com looks back at the major milestones in UK censorship history, from the 19th to the 21st centuries. What are the films that broke the mould?

1913

Due to exhibitors' fears of official intervention, The British Board of Film Censors (BBFC) is established by the film industry itself, with the promise that 'No film will be passed that is not clean and wholesome and absolutely above suspicion.' Films are given either 'U' (for universal exhibition) or 'A' (more suitable for adults) certificates.

The BBFC has no legal powers to censor films, but its advice is generally followed by local authorities, which have the power to withdraw cinema licences. This is still the case today.

1917

In response to a growing lobby in favour of state censorship, the new BBFC President, Liberal MP T P O'Connor, publishes 'O'Connor's 43' – a list of the 43 grounds on which films might be cut under the guidance of film examiners. These provide the basis for BBFC policy until World War II.

1933

The board objects to a record 504 of the 1,713 films submitted to it. Within a few years, the film industry has got the message. By the end of the 1930s only a handful of films are refused certificates each year. This is in large part due to tough new regulations in Hollywood, which crushed the early freedom of the film industry – the so-called Hays Code (named after the head of the Senate-appointed committee whose relentless sense of moral outrage was brought to bear on every film made) gave censors the power to intervene even at the scripting stage.

Even so, in 1933, the BBFC still feels it necessary to introduce an advisory 'H' classification for horror movies, indicating that such films would be unsuitable for children under 16 years of age.

1938

No Orchids For Miss Blandish is passed by the BBFC, but its violent content (tame by today's standards) prompts widespread criticism. BBFC secretary Arthur Watkins Harris formulates three principles by which the board should in future judge films:

1. Is the story, incident or dialogue likely to impair the moral standards of the public by extenuating vice or crime or depreciating moral standards?

2. Is it likely to give offence to reasonably minded cinema audiences?

3. What effect would it have on children?

1939

The outbreak of war sees responsibility for film censorship shared between the BBFC and the Ministry of Information. Pre-war rules are actually relaxed rather than tightened, presumably for the boosting of public morale. The go-ahead is given to anti-Nazi films such as *Pastor Hall*, which had been rejected before the war under rules banning films that might 'wound the susceptibilities of foreign peoples'. Also approved is *Love On The Dole*, formerly rejected as 'sordid'.

1954

The Television Act 1954 establishes commercial television and sets up the ITA (Independent Television Authority) to preside over content and decency on the new services.

1955

The Garden of Eden is the first of a rash of British films that attempt to get round the restrictions on nudity by purporting to be documentary features about naturism. Although refused certificates by the BBFC, a number of local authorities allow them to be shown. From then on, the BBFC relaxes its rules to permit 'discreet' nudity.

Parliament enacts the Obscene Publications Act, in which works are deemed obscene if they have a 'tendency to deprave and corrupt'. An important clause allows a defence based on

context and worth. Thus artworks can go beyond what is deemed otherwise commonly unacceptable. Conviction requires a jury trial.

1963

New Television Act: ITA code for programme makers gives guidance on rules for the portrayal of violence and on general standards and practice. The Authority gets stronger powers over programme schedules, ad content and timing.

1965

The BBC bans the television broadcast of *The War Game* because of its realistic depiction of the after-effects of a nuclear holocaust, including the shooting of civilians. Sony launches the CV200, the first consumer home video machine. Parliament bans cigarette advertising on television.

1967

Local authorities allow the screening of Joseph Strick's *Ulysses*, in which the word 'fuck' is spoken for the first time on British cinema screens.

1969

Ken Russell's *Women in Love* features a nude wrestling scene with Alan Bates and Oliver Reed, in which male genitals could be seen. The sequence is blurred at the insistence of the censor.

1970

Andy Warhol's *Flesh* is prosecuted for obscenity, but the case is dropped. The film is subsequently passed by the BBFC, becoming the first in Britain to show an erect penis.

1972

The 'X' certificate is changed, restricting such films to audiences aged 18 and over. At the same time, a new 'AA' category is introduced barring children under 14.

1974

The home video revolution begins. The early years, before the Government intervenes with the Video Recordings Act of 1993 and the 'video nasties' list, are something of a free-for-all: distributors can sell and rent pornography and violent exploitation without serious hindrance, beyond the cumbersome Obscene Publications Act which requires an expensive trial, and is likely to result in quixotic jury verdicts.

1975

The Texas Chainsaw Massacre is granted an 'X' certificate by the Greater London Council, despite being rejected by the BBFC. It has now been seen on British television.

1977

The new Criminal Law Act extends the Obscene Publications Act 1959 to cover film. This allows for the context and artistic merit of a film to be taken into account in determining whether or not it is obscene. This enables cuts once made to *Last Tango in Paris*, for example, to be waived.

1978

The Protection of Children Act makes it illegal to show indecent images of children in films, regardless of context, as would have been arguable under the Obscene Publications Act.

1982

The BBFC introduces the familiar classification categories of 'U', 'PG', '15', '18' and 'R18'. The additional categories of '12' and '12A' would be introduced in 1989 and 2003, respectively. The law is tightened to prevent instant membership being offered by bogus 'cinema clubs', which had provided exemption from the normal film classification system, but not from prosecution for obscenity. The R18 rating for video follows in 1985.

1985

The BBFC drops the word 'Censors' from its title, becoming the British Board of Film Classification.

1993

The killing in Liverpool of two-year-old Jamie Bulger by a pair of young boys prompts a fresh national outcry over 'video nasties'. The new Criminal Justice Act amends the Video Recordings Act 1984, requiring the BBFC to pay special attention to video representations of violence, horror, criminal behaviour, sex and drugs.

1997

Two films, once banned in the 'video nasties' era, are passed – *The Texas Chainsaw Massacre* passes uncut, while *The Driller Killer* is extensively cut. *The Exorcist* is passed for video, without cuts. However, *A Cat In The Brain*, another 'video nasty', is again rejected for its blending of sex and violence.

July 2000

The BBFC launch new guidelines for R18 releases, outlining how film and video will be classified from now on. The number of R18 videos increases dramatically. The new Guidelines spell out, for the first time, what is and is not acceptable in R18 films.

August 2000

The German feature film *Christiane F*, which depicts the realities of drug-addicted youth, passes uncut for video, despite scenes of intravenous drug use.

September 2000

The BBFC, following an ambitious survey of audience attitudes, launches a new set of Guidelines. Rules for all categories are overhauled, particularly at 18, where cuts would, in future, be rare. The BBFC publishes their research findings, with the news that audiences are more tolerant of adult content than expected, under the title *Sense and Sensibilities*.

October 2000

The Government considers abolishing the BBFC's statutory responsibility for the classification of videos and transferring them to Ofcom, the super-regulator to be created under the terms of the Communications Bill. The BBFC argues for their continued independence, citing their extensive expertise. Were the BBFC to be superseded, the Government would for the first time have taken direct responsibility for classification. The BBFC is reprieved.

June 2001

Norwich is chosen to pilot a new film classification category: PG-12 (later to be renamed 12A). This will allow parents or guardians to decide whether children younger than 12 are allowed to see certain films.

Continuing BBFC concern about glamourisation of knives and violence in *Lara Croft: Tomb Raider* results in cuts to the film in order to achieve the '12' rating that the distributor had requested. A 15 certificate would have been unlikely to attract such cuts. The film receives a 'PG-13' rating in the United States, incompatible with the usual 12 UK rating. Mission Impossible II and Charlie's Angels are other examples of 'PG-13' films appealing to the young, whose violent content is regarded as unacceptable in the UK at '12'. In those cases, the distributors opt for the more restrictive '15' rating rather than the cuts necessary for '12'.

October 2001

The Norwich pilot for the proposed new PG-12 classification progresses without a hitch. Children younger than 12, if accompanied by a responsible adult, are admitted. Unaccompanied children must be 12 or over.

Sick: The Life & Death Of Bob Flanagan, Super-Masochist is passed at '18', with cuts. This documentary charting the use of sadomasochism by a terminally ill American includes scenes of actual bodily harm. Cuts are made after advice from clinical psychologists who worry that an uncut release would invite imitation by some. The film had been seen on Channel 4 in a much shorter form.

August 2002

The BBFC rolls out the new advisory 12A category nationally. The 12, introduced for films in 1989 and videos in 1994, remains. Andreas Whittam Smith is replaced as President of the BBFC by Sir Quentin Thomas CB.

December 2002

Trainspotting is now uncut, a small snip having previously been required to a scene of intravenous drug use. In 1997, the ITC challenged Channel 4's transmission of the film uncut, and then incorporated a new rule into their Code requiring that only BBFC video versions be seen on independent licensed television (with its 'viewing in the home' test). The uncut film has subsequently been screened on Film4.

2011

Horror film *The Human Centipede II (Full Sequence)* is denied a certificate by the BBFC, claiming the film is in breach of the Obscene Publications Act. It is eventually passed with an '18' certificate, but only after 32 cuts (totalling two minutes and 37 seconds) are made. It is the 28th film since 2000 to which the Board has denied classification.

⇨ The above information is reprinted with kind permission from FilmFour. Please visit www.filmfour.co.uk for further information.

Tchaikovsky's sexuality 'downplayed' in biopic under Russia's anti-gay law

Makers of Tchaikovsky film reportedly self-censor their portrayal of the composer so as not to fall foul of Russia's new law.

By Alec Luhn

Russia's legislation banning 'gay propaganda', which has already cast a cloud over the 2014 Sochi Olympics, has now reportedly prompted local filmmakers to self-censor their portrayal of the composer Pyotr Tchaikovsky, who is widely believed to have been gay.

A partly government-funded biopic of the composer of Swan Lake, The Nutcracker and the 1812 Overture will downplay his sexuality amid the homophobic political atmosphere in Russia, which passed a law in June banning the 'propaganda of non-traditional sexual relations' among minors.

The film's screenwriter, Yuri Arabov, denied Tchaikovsky had been gay and said his script had been revised to portray the composer as 'a person without a family who has been stuck with the opinion that he supposedly loves men' and who suffers over these 'rumours', he told the newspaper *Izvestiya*.

The film's producer, Sabina Yeremeyeva, said it would not run afoul of the law against gay propaganda.

No one has been fined under the federal law, although charges have been filed under similar regional bans that preceded it. However, the revision of the Tchaikovsky script plays into concerns that the law will prompt self-censorship. The vaguely worded legislation includes fines of up to £2,000 for the 'imposition of information about non-traditional sexual relations' in the mass media.

Kirill Serebrennikov, a respected filmmaker and the artistic director of the Gogol Theatre in Moscow, announced he would film a Tchaikovsky biopic in August 2012 but told the cinema website KinoPoisk that he was having trouble finding funding due to officials' concerns about the composer's homosexuality. In July, however, the biopic became one of the films the ministry of culture decided to finance after an open competition.

Larisa Malyukova, a film columnist at the independent newspaper *Novaya Gazeta*, said that in a version of the script she saw last year, Tchaikovsky suffered over his love for a younger man. Arabov's comments, however, suggested that the portrayal of the composer as gay had been edited out of the script. The Tchaikovsky screenplay went through five revisions, and the final version 'has absolutely no homosexuality, it's entirely not about that', Arabov said.

Serebrennikov declined to comment, but Yeremeyeva denied that the five revisions were related to concerns over Tchaikovsky's sexuality. The producer said the controversy over the film's treatment of the composer's orientation was 'overblown and made up.'

Malyukova suggested that Arabov's comments are a public reaction to the political situation and do not reflect the content of the film.

'You know what kind of ministry of culture we have,' she said. 'Everyone is being careful, and he's being careful, and rightly so.'

The minister of culture, Vladimir Medinsky, said in an interview with the news site Lenta.ru in March that 'sexual preferences … shouldn't be shown, shouldn't be discussed, not on television, not in parliament, not at a rally of 500,000 people'.

The state plays a major role in financing Russian-made movies, a policy that has generated an abundance of patriotic historical films in recent years. The ministry of culture is funding 30 million rubles (£580,000) of the Tchaikovsky film's total budget of 240 million rubles, according to Yeremeyeva.

Alexander Poznansky, who has published several books on Tchaikovsky, said 'denying that he was a practising homosexual is senseless' based on the writings of the composer and his brother.

'This whole situation [with the film] is another example of the current cultural atmosphere in Russia, which makes the country a laughing stock in the eyes of the educated western public,' Poznansky said.

25 August 2013

⇨ The above information is reprinted with kind permission from *The Guardian*. Please visit www.theguardian.com for further information.

Fifty Shades of YA: should teen books have ratings?

CJ Daugherty, who writes successful novels for the YA or teenage market, wonders whether the time is right for publishers to put recommended reader ages on the backs of all children's books.

By CJ Daugherty

When writing for young people, controversies about swearing and sex are nothing new. The language in classic books such as *Tom Sawyer* and *Catcher in the Rye*, both written about children but generally read by teenagers, still upsets some parents many decades after those books were first printed.

But the issue never goes away. A recent study by Brigham Young University in America found a lot of swearing and sexual language in modern novels geared at teens – 88% of the young adult books they reviewed included at least one swear word. The implication was that those books were irresponsible. That parents should be worried. The led to some calls for a book rating system, similar to film ratings. So far this hasn't happened, but writers and publishers of teen fiction are in a difficult position.

With rumours rife that there may soon be a self-published YA erotica trend fuelled by the success of *Fifty Shades of Grey*, you can see the dilemma. I didn't know any of this when I wrote my first YA book. I just plunged in, headfirst, writing teenage characters that reflected the teens I knew. My characters swear, get drunk and sneak into each other's rooms to kiss. They make mistakes and get caught out. That book has so far been published in ten countries and I have received not one complaint from any of them about the swearing or the enthusiastic kissing scenes. In fact, my German publisher considered the sexual situations and language so mild, they made my main character one year younger (15) because they worried German teens wouldn't believe a 16-year-old girl could be so innocent.

And yet, as the second book in the series was being edited this month,

my British editor and I exchanged dozens of emails about removing swearing and references to 'blowjobs'.

I write books about characters between the ages of 16 and 18. In my experience, there are no people on the planet more likely to use the word 'blowjob'. The scene in question involves a game of 'Truth or =Dare' where, I think we can all agree the issue of oral sex tends to arise. It's not that my editor is prudish. But my book – a crossover novel intended to appeal to both teens and adults – is sold in the children's section of book stores. I've seen it on shelves next to picture books aimed at six-year-olds and that makes me uncomfortable.

Supermarkets also get anxious about this sort of thing, and tend not to stock young adult books that might raise parental eyebrows. My first book, complete with bad language, was not stocked by UK supermarkets. The swearing in my second book is modest – there were three F-words in the 400-page manuscript – but we didn't want to take any chances that those might cause problems. So we surgically removed all of them.

I can't help but think that there's something to this rating system idea. If we could guarantee only readers over 14 could buy certain books, those books could be racier – and thus more realistic. Parents would feel they had more control. But then, where do you draw the line? Is the f-word for those 14 and above, or 15? What about kissing scenes? Do first-base kissing scenes get a different age rating from those that make it to second-base?

Then there's the issue of violence… It all gets very complicated very quickly.

The US has a voluntary system where publishers print recommended reader ages on the backs of all children's books. That could be a compromise solution for the UK, as well. Then parents can just glance at the back of a book to see if their 11-year-old is buying a book intended for older teens. My US publishers have not complained about swearing in my book, because it will have a 14+ recommended reading age and in the manuscripts sent to all my foreign publishers I left in all of the strong language we took out of the UK edition. Perhaps it's time for the UK to find a system that makes parents feel safer while still allowing young people to read about characters who talk and behave like real teenagers.

22 September 2012

⇨ The above information is reprinted with kind permission from *The Telegraph*. Please visit www.telegraph.co.uk for further information.

What's okay to advertise on TV?

Alcohol, gambling – cosmetic surgery? 60% say surgery should not be able to advertise; 31% say it should.

By Hannah Thompson

Cigarettes, gambling, payday loans, abortion providers, prescription drugs and debt finance solutions should not be allowed to be advertised on television, say the majority of British adults, but other potentially controversial subjects, such as alcoholic drinks, political parties, fast food and laser surgery providers should be allowed to advertise in this way, our poll on the issue has found.

⇨ 79% say that cigarettes shouldn't be allowed to be advertised on television

⇨ Payday loans (75% said that they shouldn't be allowed), gambling (73%), personal injury lawyers (65%) and cosmetic surgery providers (63%) were almost as unpopular when it comes to TV advertising

⇨ 63% say that abortion providers should not be allowed to advertise on TV

⇨ While 54% apiece would ban TV adverts for prescription drugs and debt refinancing companies

⇨ Opinions on whether alcoholic drinks should be allowed were more split, but just slightly more people would allow them (50%) than disallow them (44%)

⇨ Similarly, a slim majority of Britons would allow laser surgery providers (54% would allow), political parties and candidates (58% allow, 36% disallow), and fast food companies (61% allow, 33% disallow) to advertise

⇨ Most accepted in the TV advert stakes were children's toys, which just 15% would ban from TV advertising compared to 79% who would allow it, and 11% who think Universities shouldn't be allowed to have TV advertising, compared to 84% who think they should.

TV adverts – what's acceptable?

The results come in light of the recent call from The British Association of Aesthetic Plastic Surgeons (BAAPS) that the advertising of cosmetic surgery procedures, such as breast enlargements, should be banned – prompting debate over what advertising content should be permissible on television.

Clearly, many of the products we asked panellists about are already highly regulated or banned from television advertising in the UK, including alcohol, tobacco products, prescription drugs and gambling – and most respondents did agree that these services should indeed be banned.

Stringent rules exist where it is judged that young people may be influenced by TV adverts, such as those for alcohol products, while television advertising of tobacco products is banned under the Tobacco Advertising and Promotion Act of 2002.

Advertising of medical products which are 'likely to lead to the use of a prescription only medicine' are also banned in the UK – but this does not cover many cosmetic surgical procedures, prompting BAAPS to call for tighter regulation of the industry.

Making surgery a commodity?

BAAPS president and plastic surgeon, Fazel Fatah has said: 'In no other area of surgery would one encounter Christmas vouchers and two-for-one offers…You don't see adverts for metal hip replacements or gall bladder operations. Advertising in cosmetic surgery feeds into the worries and insecurities in a group of vulnerable people.'

However, Dr Eamonn Butler of the Adam Smith Institute has pointed out that advertising is not the problem, because 'people do not make decisions on the strength of an advertisement alone. The advertisement alerts them to the options, then they root out the information they need.'

But Fatah compares cosmetic surgery advertising to other medicines, and was adamant that 'it is amazing that while prescription medicines cannot be advertised in magazines, invasive surgical procedures can be. These clinics have turned surgery into a commodity and that is wrong.'

6 February 2012

⇨ The above information is reprinted with kind permission from YouGov. Please visit www.yougov.co.uk.

Ofcom research on violence on TV

Ofcom has published research on consumer attitudes and trends in violence shown on UK TV programmes.

The research supports Ofcom in its role in protecting TV viewers, especially children. It looks at how violence on TV has changed since Ofcom issued guidelines to broadcasters in 2011 to avoid programmes being shown before 9pm that might be unsuitable for children.

The research comprises two separate reports. The first study focused on public attitudes towards violence on TV among people from a range of ages and socio-economic groups.

The second was an analysis of four popular UK soap operas, which looked at instances of violence, or threats of violence, and people's views on them.

Research findings

The first report, on the views of audiences, found that different demographic groups showed subtle differences in their views about violent content. However, all agreed that children should not be exposed to any sexual violence on TV before and straight after the watershed.

People considered the time of broadcast to be the single most important factor in determining the acceptability of violent content on TV. Viewers were prepared to tolerate moderately violent scenes before the watershed; however, all agreed that strong scenes with a vulnerable victim were unacceptable before 9pm.

The research also found that viewers have a sophisticated ability to analyse contextual factors when assessing whether violent scenes were acceptable. Many people said they watched violent content for a number of reasons. Some said it made genres, such as action or drama, seem realistic and provided tension, therefore contributing to their TV viewing experience.

The study of soap operas not only looked at violent scenes, but also measured those with menacing or threatening behaviour, and violence that was implied off-screen.

It found that violence in soaps was usually clearly indicated in advance, so viewers were unlikely to be surprised when it took place. The research showed 79% of violent scenes were judged 'credible' and 'rarely surprised' viewers. Broadcasters have also used violence in soap operas to help raise awareness and generate public debate around social issues such as domestic abuse.

Instances of strong scenes, portraying violence that might make the viewer uncomfortable, were very infrequent, at 6% overall. Depictions of terror during violent scenes, such as the imbalance of power in a fight, near-fatal violence and post-traumatic stress flashbacks, varied between 3% and 5% in the soaps covered.

The report also found that the amount of violence, or threats of violence, has varied over the years. *EastEnders* has shown a decline from 6.1 violent scenes per hour in 2001/2002 to 2.1 in 2013.

The level of violence in *Coronation Street* has remained fairly steady, at around three scenes per hour over the same period. There was an increase in *Emmerdale*, from 2.5 to over four scenes per hour, while *Hollyoaks* has also shown a rise, from 2.1 scenes per hour between 2001 and 2002 to 11.5 scenes per hour in 2013.

Protecting viewers

Ofcom has a duty to protect viewers, especially children, from harmful and offensive content on TV, including violence. If broadcasters show programmes that break the rules, and if the breach is serious or repeated, Ofcom can impose sanctions on broadcasters, including fines.

Ofcom has previously taken action against Channel 4 after violence in *Hollyoaks* in 2013 was aired before the watershed. Following this, Ofcom notified all its licensees about the need to ensure pre-watershed material with violent scenes was limited.

Next steps

Ofcom will use this research to update its guidance issued to broadcasters about how to deal with violence on TV. It will also be used to help inform Ofcom's decisions when investigating TV programmes with violence shown before, or soon after, the watershed.

The research findings will also be shared with broadcasters to help them better understand audience expectations about violence on TV.

17 July 2014

⇨ The above information is reprinted with kind permission from Ofcom. Please visit consumers.ofcom.org.uk for further information.

Key facts

⇨ The Universal Declaration on Human Rights (UDHR) and the International Covenant on Civil and Political Rights (ICCPR) guarantee the right to freedom of expression, both in Article 19. Freedom of expression is not only important in its own right but is also essential if other human rights are to be achieved. (page 1)

⇨ Since Hitler's death, the government of Bavaria, with the agreement of the federal government of Germany, has refused to grant anyone permission to publish a new version of *Mein Kampf*, on the basis that the book is poisonous and dangerous. (page 7)

⇨ *The DaVinci Code* by Dan Brown was banned in Lebanon in 2004. (page 9)

⇨ Age ratings for online [film and TV] content are not required by law, but are used voluntarily through a service launched by the BBFC in collaboration with the home entertainment industry in 2008. (page 12)

⇨ 82% of parents prefer to download films that are classified with the trusted BBFC age ratings, symbols and BBFCinsight information. (page 12)

⇨ Upon the implementation of the 'right to be forgotten' ruling in May 2014, within the first five weeks Google had 250,000 requests from 70,000 people to remove links. (page 16)

⇨ According to official government statements, since 2010 some 5,700 UK-based sites have been taken down, while some 1,000 overseas sites have been filtered. (page 17)

⇨ Any search for 'Tiananmen Square' or '4 June 1989' on Chinese social media Twitter-like site Weibo or its main search engine Baidu has been blocked. (page 19)

⇨ In 2009, the Vietnamese government blocked Facebook. In 2010 the government tried to launch its own social networking, go.vn, where users had to provide their full names and ID card details. (page 21)

⇨ Freedom of the press (media): of the 197 countries and territories assessed during 2013, a total of 63 (32 per cent) were rated Free, 68 (35 per cent) were rated Partly Free, and 66 (33 per cent) were rated Not Free. (page 23)

⇨ In terms of 'Free' media, the world's eight worst-rated countries are Belarus, Cuba, Equatorial Guinea, Eritrea, Iran, North Korea, Turkmenistan and Uzbekistan. (page 23)

⇨ Violence against journalists, direct censorship and misuse of judicial proceedings are on the decline in Panama, Dominican Republic, Bolivia and Ecuador, although in Ecuador the level of media polarisation is still high and often detrimental to public debate. (page 29)

⇨ One of China's most influential papers, *Southern Weekly,* stated that in 2012 1,034 news reports were revised or cancelled due to censorship. (page 31)

⇨ The BBFC's age ratings decisions are reached by consensus, with the Director, the President and the two Vice-Presidents taking ultimate responsibility. (page 32)

⇨ The British Board of Film Censors (BBFC) (now known as the British Board of Film Classification) was established in 1913 with the promise that 'No film will be passed that is not clean and wholesome and absolutely above suspicion.' (page 33)

⇨ In 1954, the Television Act 1954 establishes commercial television and sets up the ITA (Independent Television Authority) to preside over content and decency on the new services. (page 33)

⇨ In 2011, the horror film *The Human Centipede II* (Full Sequence) is denied a certificate by the BBFC, claiming the film is in breach of the Obscene Publications Act. It is eventually passed with an '18' certificate, but only after 32 cuts (totalling two minutes and 37 seconds) are made. It is the 28th film since 2000 to which the Board has denied classification. (page 35)

⇨ A recent study by Brigham Young University in America found a lot of swearing and sexual language in modern novels geared at teens – 88% of the young adult books they reviewed included at least one swear word. (page 37)

⇨ The US has a voluntary system where publishers print recommended reader ages on the backs of all children's books. (page 37)

⇨ A YouGov poll found that the majority of people surveyed think that the following should not be allowed to be advertised on TV: Payday loans (75% said that they shouldn't be allowed), gambling (73%), personal injury lawyers (65%) and cosmetic surgery providers (63%). (page 38)

⇨ A YouGov poll found that the most accepted in the TV advert stakes were children's toys, which just 15% would ban from TV advertising compared to 79% who would allow it, and 11% who think Universities shouldn't be allowed to have TV advertising, compared to 84% who think they should. (page 38)

The British Board of Film Classification (BBFC)

A body appointed by the Government to classify all video and DVD releases.

Censorship

When there are restrictions on what people can see or hear and on the information they are allowed to access, this is called censorship. By censoring something, an individual, publication or government is preventing the whole truth from coming out or stopping something from being heard or seen at all. Items may also be censored or restricted to protect vulnerable people such as children, and to prevent public offence.

Classifications

Also called age ratings. Films in cinemas and on DVD, as well as computer games, must carry a classification indicating a minimum age at which the material should be watched or played. It is a criminal offence for a retailer to supply an age-restricted DVD or game to someone below the required age.

Defamation, libel and slander

The term 'defamation' refers to false claims made about an individual or group which present them in a negative and inaccurate light. When this takes a temporary form, for example in spoken comments, it is known as slander. When defamatory comments appear in a permanent form – i.e. they are communicated in writing or via a broadcast medium such as television – it is known as libel. Libel is a civil offence and should the person or group libelled wish to do so, they can pursue a claim against the originator of the defamatory comments through the courts.

Freedom of expression

Also called freedom of speech, free speech. This is protected by Article 19 of the Universal Declaration of Human Rights, which states that: 'Everyone has the right to freedom of opinion and expression; this right includes freedom to hold opinions without interference and to seek, receive and impart information and ideas through any media and regardless of frontiers.'

Free press

A free press is one which is not censored or controlled by a government. It allows us to find out what we want to know without restrictions.

The Freedom of Information Act

The Freedom of Information Act states that there should be free access to information about the Government, individuals and businesses.

Gagging order

A ruling which prevents certain information from being made public. For example, if a court case is ongoing, the press can be prevented by law from publishing some of the details if it is felt this would affect the outcome of the case – i.e. by influencing the jury and therefore preventing the defendant from having a fair trial.

Non-violent direct action (NVDA)

Peaceful protesting. This means that an individual can take part in a public protest but it must not involve violence against property or persons.

Press Complaints Commission

The PCC is a regulatory body responsible for ensuring that UK newspapers and magazines adhere to a Code of Practice. The Code aims to ensure responsible journalism by setting down rules on matters such as accuracy in reporting, privacy intrusion and media coverage of vulnerable groups. If a member of the public is affected by unfair media coverage, they can complain to the PCC, citing which part of the Code of Practice they feel has been breached. The Code was laid down by newspaper editors themselves, and the PCC consists of representatives of the major publishers: thus the newspaper industry is self-regulating.

The watershed

The watershed is the name for the 9pm cut-off point in television scheduling, after which television channels can show programmes containing material which may not have been suitable for a younger audience, such as scenes of a sexual nature or swearing.

Assignments

Brainstorming

⇨ In small groups, discuss what you know about censorship. Consider the following points:

- What is censorship?
- What is freedom of the press?
- Why are films and TV shows censored?

Research

⇨ Over the course of a week, look at newspapers (online or in print) and count the number of stories that would not be allowed to be printed if the Government banned anything that could be seen as derogatory towards them or their values. At the end of the week, discuss with your class and consider the effect this might have on society.

⇨ Choose a country from the *Freedom of the press worldwide in 2014* map on page 28. Research censorship in that country and create a leaflet including pictures and case studies to illustrate your findings.

⇨ Choose one of the books from the banned books list on page 9 and research its history. Write some notes exploring why the book was censored and where. Feedback to your class.

Design

⇨ Design a poster that promotes freedom of the press.

⇨ Choose one of the articles in this book and create an illustration to highlight the key themes/message of your chosen article.

⇨ Choose one of the films listed in the timeline on page 33 and design a poster to promote it.

⇨ Choose one of the books from the banned books list on page 9 and design a new cover.

Oral

⇨ 'Books aimed at teenagers should be given age ratings so their parents can judge what is appropriate for them to read.' Debate this motion as a class, with one group arguing in favour and the other against.

⇨ Talk to an adult you know about how DVD, film and television censorship has changed in their lifetime. Do they think that age-ratings have been relaxed? Is there more violence on TV? Ask them for some examples and then discuss your findings with your class.

⇨ Read the article *Freedom of expression* on page 1 and create a five-minute presentation to teach 11- to 12-year-olds about the concept.

⇨ Read the article *Nothing should be censored – not even Mein Kampf* on page 6 and, in pairs, discuss the author's point of view. Do you agree or disagree? Feedback to your class.

⇨ 'People should be able to say what they want on Twitter without getting into trouble because they have a right to freedom of expression.' Discuss this statement in pairs. Do you agree?

Reading/writing

⇨ Read George Orwell's *1984* and write a review exploring how the author deals with the theme of censorship.

⇨ Research the issue of censorship in China. Write a two-page article for your school newspaper that explores the topic.

⇨ Write a blog post from the point of view of the blogger who was sentenced to 30 months in prison. Explore your feelings about your conviction, why you believe you were convicted and what you hope others around the world might do to raise awareness of Internet repression in Vietnam.

⇨ Write a one-paragraph definition of censorship.

⇨ Write an essay exploring the question: 'Is it acceptable to advertise cigarettes on television?'

⇨ Consider the theme of censorship in your answer. Write no more than two sides of A4.

⇨ Imagine the following situation: A child has been asked by their English teacher to read *Harry Potter*. Their parents feel very strongly that the book is inappropriate because of its themes of witchcraft, death and resurrection. Either:

- Write a letter from the point of view of the parent, explaining why you think the book should not be taught. Or,
- Write a letter from the point of view of the teacher, explaining why you think it would be inappropriate to prevent children from reading the book.

⇨ Watch *The Hunger Games* and write a review exploring how the director deals with the theme of censorship. (If you prefer you could read the book.)

Acknowledgements

The publisher is grateful for permission to reproduce the material in this book. While every care has been taken to trace and acknowledge copyright, the publisher tenders its apology for any accidental infringement or where copyright has proved untraceable. The publisher would be pleased to come to a suitable arrangement in any such case with the rightful owner.

Images

All images courtesy of iStock, except pages 32 and 39 © Freepik. Icon on page 41 © SimpleIcon.

Illustrations

Don Hatcher: pages 30 & 38. Simon Kneebone: pages 4 & 36. Angelo Madrid: pages 26 & 37.

Additional acknowledgements

Editorial on behalf of Independence Educational Publishers by Cara Acred.

With thanks to the Independence team: Mary Chapman, Sandra Dennis, Christina Hughes, Jackie Staines and Jan Sunderland.

Cara Acred

Cambridge

January 2015